Top Class Activities

50 short games and activities for teachers

Series Editor:
Peter Watcyn-Jones

PENGUIN BOOKS

PENGUIN ENGLISH

Published by the Penguin Group
Penguin Books Limited, 27 Wrights Lane, London W8 5TZ, England
Penguin Putnam Inc., 375 Hudson Street, New York, New York 10014, USA
Penguin Books Australia Limited, Ringwood, Victoria, Australia
Penguin Books Canada Limited, 10 Alcorn Avenue, Toronto, Ontario, Canada M4V 3B2
Penguin Books (NZ) Limited, Private Bag 102902, NSMC, Auckland, New Zealand

Penguin Books Limited, Registered Offices: Harmondsworth, Middlesex, England

10 9 8 7 6 5 4 3 2

Printed in England by William Clowes Limited, Beccles and London
Set in New Century Schoolbook and Helvetica

Acknowledgements

I am very grateful to all the authors who found the time in a busy writing schedule to submit work for this project. I am also indebted to Michael Nation at Penguin for his encouragement and enthusiasm when, at one point, the project seemed doomed to failure. Finally, I would like to thank all those authors who, although unable to contribute, were encouraging in their replies. It is to be hoped they will be able to contribute to a follow-up book.

The publishers make grateful acknowledgement to the following for permission to reproduce copyright material:

p.32, R. Carter and M.N. Long, The Web of Words, by permission of Cambridge University Press; p.32, Craig Raine, 'A Martian Sends a Postcard Home', from A Martian Sends a Postcard Home, 1979, by permission of Oxford University Press; p.36, p.37, Stephen Pile, The Book of Heroic Failures, copyright © 1979, 1989 Stephen Pile. Reproduced by permission of the author c/o Rogers, Coleridge & White Ltd, 20 Powis Mews, London W11 lJN; p.40, p.41, reproduced by permission of Oxford University Press, from Classroom Dynamics by Jill Hadfield © Oxford University Press 1992.

Every effort has been made to trace copyright holders in every case. The publishers would be interested to hear from any not acknowledged here.

CONTENTS

* E: Elementary LI: Lower intermediate I: Intermediate UI: Upper intermediate A: Advanced; +: = and above

* E: Elementary LI: Lower intermediate I: Intermediate UI: Upper intermediate A: Advanced; +: = and above

Introduction

Top Class Activities is the latest book in the Penguin series of source books for teachers. The idea for the book came while browsing through a record store one day and noticing how popular compilation albums were – Country's Greatest Hits, The Ultimate 80s Ballads, Dance 96, Rock 'n' Roll Love Songs, etc. Why not have a similar book for teaching English, I thought – a sort of 'EFL's Greatest Hits' book. The road from the initial idea to the final product has been a long and fairly difficult one, with lots of diversions, holdups, accidents and occasional dead ends. But in the end it was well worth the effort.

Top Class Activities contains a selection of 50 short games and activities written by 29 well-known EFL authors. They are varied and include vocabulary games, discussion activities, questionnaires, quizzes, role-plays, grammar and listening and reading activities. There is even an activity based on Elvis Presley's song 'Are You Lonesome Tonight?' They are suitable for mainly young adults and the difficulty ranges from elementary to advanced. They can all be completed in about 15 minutes and each game or activity contains material to be photocopied. It is hoped they will prove a useful addition to any general course as well as being an invaluable source book for busy teachers looking for exciting, short activities to use in the classroom.

The organisation of vocabulary games and activities

The activities in **Top Class Activities** are designed for pair work, group work and, occasionally, whole class activities. They have been grouped alphabetically according to author. The contents section gives details of level plus type of activity. Part 1 of the book gives detailed teacher's notes for each activity while Part 2 contains the various cards, handouts etc. to be photocopied. Where a key is necessary, this is included in the teacher's notes.

Classroom organisation

Although class sizes vary considerably, the book assumes an average class size of 10–20 students. Where possible, the classroom should be physically rearranged to facilitate working in pairs or groups. However, should this not be possible, even the more traditional front-facing rows of desks can be easily adapted for pair work and group work. For pair work, students can either work with the person sitting next to them or the person in front of or behind them. For group work, two students can easily turn their chairs round to face two others behind them. Where you have an uneven number of students in the class, most pair work activities can be done by three people (if necessary, two students against one).

The role of the teacher

For the majority of these games and activities the teacher's role is largely a passive one. The teacher is mainly responsible for:

- preparing the material in sufficient quantities
- explaining clearly what is to be done
- 'checking' answers at the end of an activity

Once an activity has started, students work independently of the teacher at their own pace. The teacher goes round the classroom listening and monitoring their progress and only interfering or helping if *absolutely necessary*.

Time-limits

Most of the activities can be done in 15 minutes. For those odd occasions where it may be possible for an activity to go on and on, it is advisable to set a time-limit and to stop the students whether they have finished or not. Apart from the obvious difficulties of students finishing at different times, the checking process is often an integral and, from the learning point of view, important part of the activity. As such it is better that you check with the whole class rather than individual groups.

Storing the material

The material to be photocopied can be divided into two types: (a) handouts which the students write on and (b) material which the students use but do not write on.

To save the teacher unnecessary work, therefore, it is a good idea that material that can be re-used should be made as durable as possible. One way is to mount everything on thin card. (Many photocopiers nowadays allow the use of card.) These cards and handouts can then be stored in separate envelopes (clearly labelled on the outside), which can be handed back to the teacher at the end of the activity.

All the activities presented in this book require preparation on the part of the teacher. It is hoped that all the extra effort will prove to be rewarding.

PART 1: TEACHER'S NOTES

1 Honestly!
Intermediate and above

Jake Allsop

Target group: *Young adult / Adult*

Type of activity: *Reading / Discussion*

The material is designed to provoke discussion by exploring the double standards that most of us live by. In particular, it is likely to bring out the following points:

- Do we do 'the right thing' because we think we will be caught if we do the wrong thing?
- Circumstances rather than our moral code determine how we behave – e.g. we will happily cheat a company (getting off a bus without paying) but not a friend.
- We might use lying for a good purpose, e.g. in order to be tactful.

It is important not to try to force conclusions from your group or class. Let them explore as far as they wish. After all, we are dealing with moral conflicts which are very hard to resolve.

Method

1 Make copies of the handout on page 28 one copy for each student. The first seven questions are a warm-up. This phase is best carried out as a whole group activity, with input of vocabulary from the teacher as needed. Initially, each student should consider each question silently, and make a written note of his/her answer before the general discussion begins.

2 The students now complete the questionnaire individually and silently. Alternatively, students can work in pairs, where each one in the pair tries to predict how the other is likely to respond.

3 Once everyone has completed the questionnaire, the questions can be opened to general discussion (there will be a lot of 'it depends' and specification of variations in the situations described). Each student is free to reveal or not reveal his/her responses.

4 There will inevitably be a clamour for the interpretation of the responses. Make and hand out copies of the 'key' on page 29. It is not meant to be more than suggestive, as, in fact, so much does depend on the interpretation of the situations described and upon factors which are not made explicit in them.

2 My word!
Lower Intermediate and above

Jake Allsop

Target group: *Young adult / Adult*

Type of activity: *Oral interaction / Vocabulary / Grammar (sentence construction)*

In this activity each student tries to score as many points as possible by continuing a story started by the teacher, using a set number of words.

Method

1 Copy the handout on page 30 – one copy for each student. Check that all the words are known.

2 Explain the rules of the game, namely that you will begin a story and then the students have to continue it using a word from the list. Here are some possible story openings:

I got on a bus the other morning to go to town. When I sat down, I noticed a strange object on the seat next to me. It was a ...

One day, my friends and I went down to the river for a picnic. We were sitting on the river bank eating our sandwiches when a woman in a uniform came up to us. She was very ...

It was midnight and John was fast asleep. Suddenly, he heard ...

3 Ask (or appoint) someone to continue. This person now has one minute in which to continue the story and to try to include as many words as possible from the list. When a word is used, any member of the class may challenge it if (s)he thinks it has been wrongly used or if (s)he thinks that it does not fit into the story. If the word is allowed, it is crossed off and the student gains the number of points next to it. A new student now carries on. (Clearly the task gets harder – and usually more hilarious – as the words are used up.) Stop the activity after 10–15 minutes and count scores.

Follow-up

1 The class can be set the task of writing the story as told (relying on their memories).

2 The teacher can give an arbitrary list of 6–10 words and ask the students to construct a story involving these words. (This can also be used as a warm-up.)

3 Telling a story
Intermediate and above

Jan Bell and Roger Gower

Target group: *Young adult / Adult*

Type of activity: *Speaking*

This activity combines problem solving and story telling. Students should be encouraged to use their imaginations.

Method

1 Copy and cut out the objects and the problems on page 31 – one set for each group.

2 Explain the rules. Each group must select five of the objects without looking at the situations.

They then turn over one of the situations and select three of the objects they have chosen (no more, no less) to tell the story.

3 When they have worked out how to complete the story the students should be asked to practise saying the whole of the story using past verb forms.

4 Students can then be asked to tell the story to the other groups. The class can then decide which story they think is best.

Variations

1 The stories can be mimed and the other groups can guess what the story was.

2 Groups can tell one story or more than one story.

3 Different groups can be asked to tell different stories.

4 Stories can be recorded and another group can make suggestions for improvement. The stories can then be re-recorded.

Acknowledgement: The idea is based on the 'Think Links' ideas by Edward de Bono.

4 Reading different worlds *Advanced*

Ron Carter

Target group: *Young adult / Adult*

Type of activity: *Reading / Writing / Literature / Language awareness*

This is an exercise in comparing and contrasting two thematically similar texts written for very different purposes. The main aim is to enable learners to reflect on different uses of language by reading, and by reading opening their way into writing.

Method

1 Divide the class into pairs or groups of 4–5 students.

2 Copy and cut out the two texts (A and B) on page 32 – one set for each pair or group. Also copy and cut out the student question sheet on page 33.

3 Give out text B first. Allow the students time to read it, then hand out text A. Again, allow them time to read it. Finally hand out the question sheet. Allow them 10–15 minutes to answer the questions. The students should consider the following:

- that different print sizes signal different levels of importance to the message.
- that in the poem the aim is for the reader gradually to work out what the object is.
- that 'soothing to sleep with sounds' = talking into the earpiece; 'tickling' = dialling.

4 Students can get together with another pair or group to compare and discuss their answers.

Follow-up questions (for whole class)

1 Text A does not contain any metaphors or ambiguous words. Why not?

2 If you read text A without a telephone in front of you or in your hand, would it matter?

3 If you read text B without a telephone in front of you, would it matter?

4 Why is the word 'telephone' not mentioned in text B?

Writing task (Optional extra)

Students working individually can try their hand at writing. Copy the handout on page 34 – one copy for each student. They can either do it in class or it can be set for homework.

Acknowledgement: This activity is developed from *The Web of Words: Exploring Literature through Language* by Ronald Carter and Michael N Long (Cambridge University Press, 1987).

5 Cardversations *Intermediate/Advanced*

Julian Edge

Target group: *Adult*

Type of activity: *Communication activity*

This is a conversation/discussion game for small groups.

Method

1 Copy the handout on page 35 – one copy for each student. Check the expressions are understood.

2 One student names a topic – anything will do (e.g. learning a language, how to slim, violence, etc.).

3 The student to his/her left 'plays' the opening 'card' by saying, *The first thing is that ...* and completing the sentence appropriately.

4 Students take turns to the left, playing any card they wish except the closing card. Set a (five-second) limit, or the turn passes. Each card can be played only once.

5 When all other cards have been played, the next student must play the closing card.

NOTES

a If possible, use a tape of competent speakers playing the game as an introduction.

b Use stick-on address labels to expand the range of expressions used on further handouts.

Variations

When students are used to the above method, many variations are possible:

1 Cut the sheets up into actual 'cards' and deal them to be played unseen.

2 Appoint an observer to feed back on appropriacy and accuracy.

3 Withdraw the fixed sequence of turns and invite students to play competitively.

Acknowledgement: There is more information about

the game and ideas for cards in: 'Cardversations' (World Language English 3/3: 190–195,1984.)

6 Inserting words

Intermediate

Simon Greenall

Target group: *Young adult / Adult*
Type of activity: *Writing / Reading*

This activity involves a lot of reading but because it also focuses on word order, it is a good writing practice as well, without actually having to write anything down.

Method

1 Make copies of the handout on page 36 – one copy for each student.
2 Ask them to decide where the missing words go in the passage. They will have to read the passage several times before they can do this successfully.
3 Correct the students' answers orally.

Key

As they were taking him to the airport in a ***police*** *car ...*

By chance the policeman came from Naples and replied ***fluently*** *in Italian.*

Because he hadn't visited Italy since he was a ***small*** *child ...*

... but he thought they were delayed by the ***heavy*** *Roman traffic.*

He needed to find his way to the ***bus*** *station.*

He thought he had ***already*** *arrived in Rome.*

You may find that some students find possible alternatives. If they are syntactically correct, then accept them.

Follow-up

1 Tell them you 'invented' the words, and they don't really belong to the passage. Choose a new passage, either one from your textbook, or one you have recently looked at in class. Ask the students to work in pairs.
2 Working separately, ask the students to 'invent' five or six words which can go into the new passage. Ask them to write them on a separate piece of paper.
3 Ask the students to exchange pieces of paper and to decide where the words go in the new passage. If Student A can find more than one suitable position for each of Student B's words, Student A gets a point. The student with highest number of points is the winner.

7 Deleting words

Intermediate

Simon Greenall

Target group: *Young adult / Adult*
Type of activity: *Writing / Reading*

Like Activity 6, Inserting words, this is also a reading activity which focuses on word order.

Method

1 Make copies of the handout on page 37 – one copy for each student.
2 Explain that the text has a number of words which can be crossed out, and the general sense remains. Ask the students to read the passage and to cross out five words which are not necessary to the general sense of the passage. Point out that they cannot cross out two or more words together. For example, you cannot cross out:
   On a flight across America ~~in 1976~~.
3 Find out how many students found more than five words.

Key (suggestion)

On a flight across America in 1976, a man rose from his seat, took out a ~~hand~~ gun and pointed it at the ~~air~~ hostess.

'Take me ~~immediately~~ to Detroit,' he said ~~quietly~~.

'We're ~~already~~ going to Detroit,' she replied ~~calmly~~.

'~~Oh~~ ... good,' he said and sat down ~~again~~.

Follow-up

Choose a new passage, either one from your textbook, or one you have recently looked at in class. Ask the students to look for any words which are not necessary. Remind them that they cannot cross out two or more words together.

8 Predicting from check questions

Intermediate

Simon Greenall

Target group: *Young adult / Adult*
Type of activity: *Writing / Reading*

This is an activity where students attempt to predict a story before they have actually read it by making up answers to a given set of questions based on the story.

Method

1 Make copies of the questions on page 38 and of the passage on page 39 – one copy for each student. To begin with, hand out copies of the questions.
2 Explain that they are going to reconstruct a passage called *A weekend to remember* from the check questions before they have read the

passage itself. Reassure them that there is a lot they will be able to predict, but if there is anything which they are not sure about, they should leave a blank. They will have to fill in the blank with the missing information.

For speaking and listening practice, ask the students to do this in pairs.

3 Now hand out copies of the actual passage. Ask the students to read it and to fill in the blanks with any missing information.

---

9 Medals *Elementary and above*

Jill Hadfield

Target group: *Young adult / Adult*

Type of activity: *Course ending / Morale boosting*

This is an activity which will boost morale and create positive feelings. It is good for the end of term, to round a course off, or mid-term to give people a lift and dispel the mid-term blues.

Method

1 Copy and cut out the medal outlines on page 40. Prepare enough for every student in the class to have one to give away and one to keep. Make one for yourself too. You will also need a bag of coloured pens and pins.

2 Make yourself a medal saying, *Long-suffering Mother* or *Good Friend* or *Patient Teacher* or some other quality you feel deserves recognition. Wear it to class.

3 Explain to the students that you thought you weren't getting enough recognition, so you thought you'd award yourself a medal. Tell them you think it's time for a bit of general recognition all round, so you've decided on a medal ceremony.

4 Give out the blank medals, two per student.

5 Ask them to make a medal for themselves, and for the person on their right, honouring them for some quality they possess. They can spread out a bit at this point, to work on their medals in secret. Pass around the coloured pens and crayons.

6 When everyone has finished, have a medal ceremony with as much pomp and circumstance as possible (solemn music, if practicable). Students should come forward one at a time to receive their decorations.

Acknowledgement: This activity first appeared in *Classroom Dynamics* by Jill Hadfield (Oxford University Press, 1992).

---

10 Remember when ... *Elementary and above*

Jill Hadfield

Target group: *Young adult / Adult*

Type of activity: *Course ending / Morale boosting*

This is an activity which will boost morale and create positive feelings. It is good for the end of term in those last days where students come to class but don't feel like any serious work. It rounds a course off nicely.

Method

1 Copy and cut out the handout on page 41 – one pile of strips for each student.

2 Ask the class to think back over the term and to try and remember nice or funny things that have happened to the group during the term.

3 Ask them to complete the sentence slips in as many ways as possible.

4 After they have been writing a little while, join them up with a partner and ask them to share their sentences. Then ask them to go on writing, jogging each others' memories.

5 Finally, ask everyone in the class to share their memories.

Follow-up

It is a good idea if you have time, to collect all the sentences, type them up and make a souvenir booklet for everyone in the class.

Acknowledgement: This activity first appeared in *Classroom Dynamics* by Jill Hadfield (Oxford University Press, 1992).

---

11 Musical stories *Intermediate*

Jeremy Harmer

Target group: *Young adult / Adult*

Type of activity: *Creative writing*

This is a 'creative' writing activity which depends on having tapes of two very different mood musical extracts. (Each extract should last for no more than 3 minutes.)

Method

1 Copy the handout on page 42 – one copy for each student.

2 Tell the students that you are going to play them some music. They are going to continue the story in any way they can, but they should let the music tell them what to write.

3 Wait until they are all ready and then start the tape.

4 When the tape has finished, give them a short time to finish their stories.

5 Tell the students to turn their pages upside down.

6 Tell them that once again you are going to play them some music. They are going to continue the story in any way they can and again they should let the music tell them what to write.

7 Play the second tape. When it has finished give them a short time to finish their stories.

8 Tell the students to give their papers to another student. Allow them time to read the stories they have been given.

9 Ask the students to read out one of the stories they have in front of them (not their own stories). The rest of the class should try to guess whether the story was written under the influence of the first piece of music or the second.

Acknowledgement: As with most of the musical activities I use this was provoked by reading *Musical Openings* by David Cranmer and Clermont Leroy, (Longman Pilgrims). Two pieces of music that have worked well for me are *Tchaikovsky's 1st string quartet* (2nd movement) for the first piece of music and *Beanfields* by the Penguin Café Orchestra for the second.

12 You *Elementary and above*

Jeremy Harmer

Target group: *Primary / Adult*

Type of activity: *Creative writing*

This is an activity which makes even the most recalcitrant student into a poet!

Method

1 Copy the handout on page 43 – one copy for each student.

2 Tell the students to think of somebody they either love or hate. It can be a member of their family, girlfriend/boyfriend, a work colleague, a fellow student, etc.

3 Tell the students to write about the person they have thought of as if they were a type of food. Give them (simple) examples:

You are a chocolate ice-cream.

You are a loaf of garlic bread.

Give them time to write a line.

4 Tell the students to write the next line as if their person is a kind of weather. Once again be prepared to give examples:

You are a hot summer day.

You are an autumn mist.

5 Go through all the lines giving examples if you think it is necessary. The tone of your voice – the type of silence you create while students are writing – is crucial to the success of this activity.

6 When the students have finished have them swap their papers. They can now (if they want to) read out the poem they have in front of them to the rest of the class.

Acknowledgement: I was first persuaded about the success of this activity by the work of Maura Dooley published in *Poets Live* by the Eastern Arts Association in the UK.

13 Numbers quiz *Elementary/Intermediate**

Deirdre Howard-Williams

Target group: *All*

Type of activity: *Quiz / Vocabulary*

This is a fun activity based on trying to work out various 'mystery expressions' all based on numbers. It can be done individually or in pairs/groups.

Method

1 Write the example (7 D in a W) on the board as a 'mystery expression' and see if the group can work out what it means. Give the answer (7 days in a week) and explain that they are going to be given a list of similar expressions to work out. You may like to set up a scoring system and ask students to work individually or in pairs or small groups.

2 Copy the handout on page 44 – one for each student, pair or group. Set a time limit or ask those who complete the first ten to stand up. Those who finish early can be encouraged to work out the harder examples. Finally, everyone can be asked to think up two number expressions of their own.

3 Check orally, giving clues for any expressions that nobody was able to work out. Allocate points and listen to the examples the students have made up. Give extra points for particularly good ones or ones that the group had difficulty with.

Key

1 *12 months in a year*
2 *52 weeks in a year*
3 *26 letters in the alphabet*
4 *24 hours in a day*
5 *100 pence in a pound*
6 *30 days in September*
7 *60 seconds in a minute*
8 *100 years in a century*
9 *10 years in a decade*
10 *4 seasons in a year*
11 *The 5 senses*
12 *10 Downing Street*
13 *12 signs of the zodiac*

There are of course plenty more!

2001 S O (*2001 Space Odyssey*) and the 10 C (the *10 Commandments*) to name but two.

* With Intermediate groups place more emphasis on the harder examples and on them inventing their own expressions.

14 Wish you were here *Elementary and above*

Deirdre Howard-Williams

Target group: *All*

Type of activity: *Vocabulary connected with holiday activities / Asking questions*

In this activity students complete holiday postcards for each other.

Method

1 Briefly introduce the subject of holidays and sending postcards (a real postcard could be used as an example).

2 Copy the handout on page 45 – one for each student.

3 Set the scene: they are on holiday and are sending a postcard to a friend. They have to fill in the spaces on the postcard (using gerunds and nouns). Give a few examples and be ready to help lower level groups with vocabulary. Stress that they must not sign the postcard.

4 Everyone now works individually to complete their postcard. It is not necessary for them to write a P.S. The function of the P.S. is to give something extra for the quick workers to do if they show signs of getting bored while waiting for others to finish. While the students are working, circulate to give help with vocabulary and to make sure that no one signs their name.

5 Take in all the postcards and redistribute them. Explain that everyone has now received a mystery card in the post and the aim is to find out who sent it.

6 Students walk around the room asking one another questions to find out who sent the card they now have. For an elementary class, questions would be simple questions requiring a yes/no answer, e.g. *Do you go windsurfing? / Do you like barbecues?* etc. For an intermediate class, questions could avoid using the actual vocabulary on the card and be more indirect (like a detective), e.g. *Do you like water sports? / Do you like eating in the open air?* etc.

7 When students think they have found the person who sent them a postcard, they give it back to them. If it is correct, the sender signs and keeps it. If incorrect, they keep on trying. Once students have their original postcard back and have also found out who wrote to them and given that postcard back, they have finished and may sit down.

8 Those who have finished can write a P.S. The most amusing and original ones can be read out to the class.

15 The chicken licken story

Elementary and above

Annie Hughes

Target group: *Primary*

Type of activity: *Listening / Speaking*

This is a story that can be followed and each cut-out character is added as it appears in the story. The children can also easily and quickly join in with the story.

Method

1 Give each child a copy of the handout on page 46 and ask them to carefully cut out the strip from the bottom of the page with all the birds on it.

2 Now ask them to carefully cut out all these birds, around the dotted lines.

3 Ask them to look at the picture on the handout and then tell them to look at the little chick on the road. Tell them that it is 'chicken licken'.

4 Now show them the cut-out birds and introduce the names for them one by one:

 1 the hen – 'henny penny'

 2 the duck – 'ducky lucky'

 3 the goose – 'goosey loosey'

 4 the turkey – 'turkey lurkey'

 5 the cockerel – 'cocky locky'

 6 the fox – 'foxy loxy'

 It would be useful to show the class a picture of a king too.

5 Now tell them to listen to the story and add each character as they hear them in the story. Show them how to add a character after 'chicken licken' on the road so that it looks as though they are walking down the road in a line. As you tell the story hold up the cut-out of the relevant character to help the pupils. As you tell the story encourage the children to join in with all the repeated dialogue as each bird joins the line!

Follow-up

This story lends itself very nicely to role-play.

1 Ask the class to help you tell the story while seven of them play the characters including chicken licken.

2 Split the class into groups of seven. Each child in a group is then given the name of a character and mimes the story as you read it out. Encourage them to repeat what the characters say.

16 It's written in the stars

Intermediate and above

Annie Hughes

Target group: *Young adult / Adult*

Type of activity: *Reading / Writing / Speaking*

This is an activity for pairs based on horoscopes.

Method

1 Organize the class into pairs, A and B. But to begin with, students work individually.

2 Give each student a copy of handout (1) on page 48, plus a copy of the *personality profile chart* on page 49. Each student now fills in the first handout choosing appropriate words from the various sections of the *personality profile chart*. Set a time-limit of about 8–10 minutes. When they have finished, they exchange papers.

3 Copy and hand out the horoscope on page 50 (one copy for each student). Using their partner's filled in form, they now try to work out which star sign best suits him/her. To make it easier to check, they could circle the corresponding words their partner chose in the various sections of the horoscope.

4 They now check by asking their partner for his/her date of birth. Was anyone true to their star sign or were most people way out?

5 Have a class discussion on horoscopes. How many believe in them? Is it possible to tell a person's character from his/her star sign?

Acknowledgement: This is a variation of an activity which is to be found in *Treasure Trail 4* by Annie Hughes and Kim Brown (Penguin Books, 1994).

17 Can you see it? – Can you make it out?

Intermediate

Roy Kingsbury

Target group: *Teenager / Young adult*

Type of activity: *Vocabulary (phrasal verbs)*

This is a 'rewriting' game for pairs or small groups.

Method

1 Copy the handout on page 51 – one copy for each pair/group.

2 Explain the rules as follows:

Under each sentence students must write a sentence which means the same, but which uses a phrasal verb chosen from those in the oval at the top of the page.

3 Set a time limit (e.g. 5 minutes) and check orally. To avoid cheating, let the students mark one another's handouts.

4 Each answer (or phrasal verb 'translation') will be clearly correct or incorrect. If correct, students gain the number of points shown in brackets after the verb.

5 At the end, fill in and total the number of points for all the correct verbs.

6 The pair or group with the highest score wins.

Key (and points)

*1 Can you **work it out**? (5 points)*

*2 You're **making it all up**! (5 points)*

*3 The weather was so bad they had to **call the game off/call off the game**. (10 points)*

*4 We've been **held up** in heavy traffic. (10 points)*

*5 That telephone receptionist **cut me off**. (10 points)*

*6 My uncle used to smoke, but he has finally **given it up**. (10 points)*

*7 Now that he can talk, they just can't **shut him up**. (10 points)*

*8 Can you help me **blow up these balloons/blow these balloons up**? (10 points)*

*9 He was **brought up** in London. (15 points)*

*10 They often **run him down**. (15 points)*

Possible maximum score: 100 points

Follow-up

At the end, if there is still 'time to kill', students might be asked to write short sentences with the phrasal verbs that are left, showing how they are used in English.

18 Home!

Upper Intermediate / Advanced

Roy Kingsbury

Target group: *Young adult / Adult*

Type of activity: *Reading / Grammar*

This is a speed-reading and reordering game for pairs.

Method

1 Copy the handout on page 52 – one copy for each pair. (Although students can work with a single sheet of paper, you might cut up the sheet into paragraphs as indicated so that students can try laying them out physically in different orders. They may find the task easier this way.)

2 Explain the rules: they must read the paragraphs and reorder them to make a sensible story as quickly as they can. They can write the order numbers of paragraphs(1 – 7) in the boxes.

3 Ten minutes must be the absolute time-limit, but one pair should have won by then.

4 Check the order of the paragraphs: it will be clearly correct or incorrect. (If a pair thinks they have won, but you find that the order they have is wrong, they are barred from correcting and shouting again.)

5 The pair that shouts 'Home!' first, and that has the paragraphs of the story in the correct order, wins.

Key

The correct order of the paragraphs:

1 C; 2 G; 3 F; 4 A; 5 D; 6 B; 7 E

Follow-up

Ask the students to try and explain why they thought paragraph C came before paragraph G, why F followed G, etc.

19 Nonsense! *Upper Intermediate/Advanced*

Roy Kingsbury

Target group: *Young adult / Adult*

Type of activity: *Reading / Grammar*

This is a reading comprehension game for students working on their own or in pairs.

Method

1 Copy the handout on page 53 – one copy for each student or pair.

2 Explain the rules as follows:

Students must read each sentence and decide and mark

A whether it makes common sense,

B whether it is totally ridiculous – nonsense! or

C whether it makes sense, but somehow sounds strange – philosophical.

3 Set a time limit (e.g. 5 minutes) and check orally. To avoid cheating, let students exchange and mark one another's handouts.

4 Each answer will be clearly Sensible, Nonsense or Philosophical. Students get 5 points for each answer marked correctly according to the key below.

5 At the end, the 'markers' add up the points for correct answers and write down the total number of points scored.

6 The student or pair with the highest score wins.

Key

The correct answers are:

1 A, 2 C, 3 B, 4 B, 5 A, 6 A, 7 B, 8 C, 9 A, 10 B, 11 C, 12 B, 13 B, 14 B, 15 A

(Maximum score possible = 75 points.)

Follow-up

Ask students to try to produce more sentences for each other which they know are nonsense, 'philosophical' or perfectly correct.

20 Word array *Intermediate and above*

Alan Maley

Target group: *Young adult / Adult*

Type of activity: *Writing / Grammar*

This is an exercise in guided creative composition. It is done in three separate stages.

Method:

Stage 1

1 Copy and cut up the *Word array* handout plus the original text on page 55 – one copy for each student. At this stage only give out the *Word array* handout.

2 Students, working individually, write their own sentences. You may need to check that they are following the instructions, that is, not adding words or changing them. Allow approximately 8–10 minutes for this stage.

3 They now work in groups of 3–4 and read out and compare their sentences. Encourage them to add/copy interesting sentences from their partners' lists. They should also check on the grammatical accuracy of their sentences.

Stage 2

1 Each group chooses sentences from their three lists which can be used to write a text – either a story or a poem. (If a group finishes early, tell them to try writing a second text.)

2 Give each group the opportunity to read its text aloud for the others in the class, but do not insist if they are too shy to do so.

Stage 3

1 Hand each group a copy of the original text. They should now compare their texts with the original. They may find that they wrote sentences which are identical to those in the original.

2 Ask the whole class now for their comments on the activity. Was it easy, difficult? How many sentences did they write which were close or identical to the original? How difficult was the fact that they were not allowed to add or change words?

Acknowledgement: The text is by Leszek Szkutnik, a well-known Polish textbook writer. The activity is an adaptation of one from *Short and Sweet 1* by Alan Maley (Penguin Books, 1994).

21 Mining a text *Upper intermediate/Advanced*

Alan Maley

Target group: *Young adult / Adult*

Type of activity: *Writing*

This is a creative writing exercise within a framework of support.

Method:

1 Copy and cut out the texts on page 56. Give each student a copy of one of the texts.

2 Students read their text carefully, then underline up to *ten* words or phrases which strike them as important in some way – perhaps because of the imagery, or their importance to the story, etc.

3 They now write down these words/phrases on a *separate piece of paper*. When they have done this, collect up all the original texts, so they cannot refer back to them.

4 Tell them that they must now use their selection of words/phrases as the basis for writing a completely *new* text. This may be a piece of narrative or a poem, a letter, a diary entry, a newspaper article, or any other text type they choose. Make sure they understand that the purpose is to create a completely *new* text, not to try to reconstruct the original from the fragments they have 'mined'. Set a time-limit (approximately 10–15 minutes).

5 They now work in pairs or groups of three. They read out their texts and their partners try to suggest modifications or improvements.

6 If there is time, some students can be asked to read their texts aloud. Otherwise, it is a good idea to pin up the texts on a wall or display board for others to read.

Acknowledgement: The texts are taken from *Campbell's Crossing and Other Short Stories* by Alan Maley (Penguin Books, 1994). The idea is a development on one in *The Inward Ear* by Alan Maley and Alan Duff (Cambridge University Press, 1989).

---

22 Welcome to Raach! *Intermediate and above*

Alan McConnell-Duff

Target group: *Young adult / Adult*

Type of activity: *Role-play / Writing*

This is a role play activity for small groups which involves the writing and delivering of the opening words of a speech.

Method

1 Copy the handout on page 57 – one copy for each group.

2 Ask the students to form groups of four and to think of an interesting title for an international conference or meeting. (The title does not have to be serious – it can be as imaginative as they wish.)

3 While the groups are discussing this, give out the handout.

4 Now tell the class that an international conference is to be held in their town. The Mayor of the town will give the welcoming address. (S)he would like to include at least two 1–2 line quotations in the opening words. The quotation must be taken from the handout.

5 Each group now takes the topic upon which it has already decided as the theme for the conference. Their task is (in approximately 10 minutes) to work out the opening lines of the Mayor's speech including at least two quotations in English. The speech should be about ten sentences long.

6 It is now time for the presentation. In each group, one person now acts as the Mayor, and in turns, each 'Mayor' presents his/her welcoming speech.

NOTE: A monolingual version of this activity was first carried out in Raach (Austria) at the end of a teacher-training course. In this version, the speech is worked out in the students' mother tongue, but still including a quotation in English. During the presentation stage, one student in each group now acts as interpreter, giving an 'off-the-cuff' translation into English.

---

23 Mean with meaning *Intermediate and above*

John McRae

Target group: *Young adult / Adult*

Type of activity: *Reading / Vocabulary*

This is a group activity which can be used after any reading class. If used regularly it will help students overcome teacher-dependence for vocabulary, and get them thinking about vocabulary for themselves. Whatever kind of text is presented, at any level, the focus of the reading class can be themes, processes, issues, etc. rather than on vocabulary as such.

It is an awareness raising exercise, as well as a useful learning game. It involves learning about the language, while acquiring some new vocabulary and reading skills.

Method

1 Copy the handout on page 58 – one copy for each student*. Either read the text to the students or let them read it themselves. Then arrange the class into groups of 3–4 students.

2 Each group now lists all the unfamiliar or unknown vocabulary items in the text that has been read.

3 They then discuss which of these items can be guessed or worked out for meaning in context. In this way some 'problem' items can be eliminated from the list. The remaining vocabulary items are now to be listed in order of importance. They put them in either the 'Need to know' column, the 'Would like to know' column or in the 'Don't need to know' column.

4 After discussion, the group reports back on the **one** item that group members really need to know. Frequently, different groups will come up with different items they need to know. This can lead to other groups saying why they did not need to know that particular item.

Variations

1 The teacher can play the game as 'mean with meaning' by only explaining one word per group, instructing the class to look up further items and report back at the next lesson.

2 Each group's Top Three might be given, according to the level of the class, the text, and the success of the elimination/reasoning which has led to the choice of the Top Three items.

*NOTE: This text is only intended as a suggestion. Any other text can be used, if preferred.

---

24 Ben Battle *Intermediate and above*

John McRae

Target group: *Young adult / Adult*

Type of activity: *Text reconstruction*

This is a text reconstruction exercise for the whole class based on a short poem. It is an exercise for both visual and verbal memory, as well as for several good grammar points, punctuation, and even the rhythm of the text.

Method

1 Make an OHP transparency of the poem on page 59.

2 Flash the text on an OHP for one short reading. It is better to *read* the text aloud with the class. Then switch it off! The point is to see how much of the text students can reconstruct after this first deliberately brief exposure. For this reason it is important **not** to warn the students what they are going to do.

3 Check that the basic pun (arms) has come across. Then ask how many lines there were, and what the man's name was. Then ask the students, working in pairs or small groups, to see how much of the story they can reconstruct. Get them to do this in writing.

4 After a few minutes, during which some students will be able to reconstruct a fair amount of the text, some just a little, the teacher begins to rewrite the text on the board. Start with the name, four blank lines, and the last word, namely:

Ben Battle ____ ____ ____ ____,
____ ____ ____ ____ ____
____ ____ ____ ____ ____ ____ ____
____ ____ ____ ____ ____ *arms.*

Work back to verbs in the last line. Explore possible choices – put down, laid down. (Check on various lay/lie confusions.) Leave the linker – 'so' or other possibilities – till later.

Do the same with the third line. Explore various possible verbs – blew off, shot off, etc. You can even play with spellings, blue off, for example. The class can then challenge the teacher's spelling!

Move to the first line, looking for verb and adjective. Is the adjective better before or after the noun? Why?

The second line should be handled last, as it is probably the one students will have had least success in reconstructing. This is because it has fewer actual content elements of the story than the other lines. Also the 'used to' form might lead students to follow it with a verb. Work back from 'arms' in line four to try out possible rhymes.

Finally look at linkers, and punctuation.

NOTE: The object is **not** to arrive at the same text as was first shown, but to explore some possibilities including short term memory!

---

25 What do you do with this? *Intermediate*

Terry Moston

Target group: *Secondary / Adult*

Type of activity: *Vocabulary / Dictionary work / Reading comprehension*

This is a word-meaning guessing game for pairs or groups. The students will also need an English-English dictionary.

Method

1 Copy and cut up the handout and the key on page 60. Each student gets a copy of the handout. The students can work in pairs or groups of 3–4. They read out the questions in turn and each person writes down his/her answers without conferring with the others in the group.

2 After all eight questions have been dealt with in this way, one person acts as compère. Give each compère a copy of the answer key. The compère reads out each question and asks each member of the group to declare their answers in public. The compère then reads out the correct definition from the key. The group decides on the basis of the correct definition which of the three uses *a*, *b* or *c* is correct.

3 Having found out which use was correct, the compère then reports to those group members who chose different uses to what they have actually said. (You said you put a tureen in your pocket.)

4 If students decide to do the follow-up activity and create their own quizzes, they could work as a group and then quiz another group. Quizzes can be written on the board, put on to an overhead transparency or written out as a worksheet and then duplicated. The quizmakers should keep a record of the correct answers. A compère or the teacher can explain the funny responses.

Key

1c, 2c, 3b, 4a, 5b, 6c, 7a, 8b

Follow-up

Make your own quiz. (*See handout*)

26 Funny face *Elementary*

Terry Moston

Target group: *Secondary / Adult*

Type of activity: *Drawing / Following written instructions / Speaking (expressing opinions)*

This is a drawing activity which tests the students' ability to follow written instructions. Each student will need a pencil and paper.

Method

1 Divide the class into pairs. Give each student a copy of the handout on page 61. This contains detailed written instructions for constructing a drawing of another student. Using these simple steps, even people who think they have no talent for drawing can produce reasonable results. Before they start, make sure that the students understand the words 'vertical' and 'horizontal'.

2 The students all work on their drawings at the same time. Remind them **not** to show their partner their drawing yet!

3 When the drawings are completed, they are exchanged for comment. It may be best if students take turns at giving their comments. While one person is commenting, the other drawing can be placed face down on the desk. (With certain learners, however, this may be counterproductive since it suppresses spontaneity.)

4 The expressions given cover common reactions. It may be necessary for the teacher to be ready to expand on these ad hoc.

Follow-up

1 All the drawings can be pinned up on the walls as a sort of Art Exhibition. The students try to say who the people are. If the teacher feels it would be useful, students can comment on the drawing once the person has been identified, using the same expressions as in 4 above.

2 Drawing the teacher is always a favourite. Maybe build in a delay of a week or two in order to consolidate the expressions.

3 The teacher writes a set of instructions for drawing abstract shapes or scenes. The students follow the instructions and compare their results.

4 The students can write their own instructions to each other for drawing an abstract shape or a scene. The author draws the shape away from the group and conceals it. They then compare the accuracy of the group's drawings.

27 A parallel exercise *Elementary and above*

Robert O'Neill

Target group: *Young adult / Adult*

Type of activity: *Reading / Speaking*

In this activity students make comparisons between themselves and two imaginary people – Constance Sunshine and Harry Chest.

Method

1 Copy the handout on page 62 – one copy for each student.

2 Read through the text and allow them time to think of their answers.

3 Each student then gets together with a partner and they take it in turns to talk about themselves and how different they are to Constance Sunshine and Harry Chest.

4 If necessary, one or two students can be asked to tell the whole class about how they differ from Constance and Harry.

Follow-up

The students can be asked to write up the differences for homework.

28 What do you think is the rest of the story? *Lower intermediate and above*

Robert O'Neill

Target group: *Young adult / Adult*

Type of activity: *Reading / Discussion*

In this activity, students are given two texts which are only fragments of a story. From these fragments they answer a series of questions – most of which are open-ended and will challenge their creativity and imagination.

Method

1 Copy the handout on page 63 – one copy for each student.

2 Either read through the two extracts with the whole class or allow them to read it themselves.

3 Arrange the class into pairs or groups of three and allow them to go through the questions after each extract.

4 Check orally, asking various pairs/groups for their answers.

Follow-up

You can ask the students to write an extra paragraph for each extract for homework. They can choose to write the paragraph that comes before the extract or after it.

29 They always talk about the weather

Intermediate

Gillian Porter Ladousse

Target group: *All*

Type of activity: *Reading / Speaking / Writing / Vocabulary*

This is a ranking exercise, followed by a writing activity.

Method

1 The students work in pairs – A and B. Give each pair a copy of the Beaufort Wind Scale on page 64. Also copy and cut the handout on page 65 in half. Give Student A and Student B his/her list of descriptions.

2 Tell the students that, working together, they have to rank the descriptions in order of the strength of the wind and write them on their grids. They can read out their descriptions but they are not allowed to look at each other's cards. Set a time limit of 5 minutes, and, if appropriate, run the activity as a competition with the pair which finishes first as the winners.

3 If there is time, or for homework, ask the students to write the descriptions in their own words from their own first-hand or second-hand experience. Encourage creative, original or humorous ideas. You can compile a class wind scale with the best ideas.

Examples

0 You can't breathe and it's very hot.

12 Ships at sea sink.

Key (A = Student A; B = Student B)

0 A – d; 1 A – e; 2 B – b; 3 A – b; 4 B – f; 5 A – a; 6 A – f; 7 B – a, 8 B – d; 9 A – c; 10 B – c; 11 B – e; 12 A – g and B – g.

Follow-up

1 Weather sayings

Write one or two weather sayings on the blackboard, such as *Red sky at night, shepherd's delight. Red sky in the morning, shepherd's warning* or *Lightning never strikes in the same place twice* or *When the wind is from the northwest, it's a good time to do business.* Ask the students if they think there is any truth in them. If so, why? Then ask them about weather sayings in their own country or countries.

2 Writing

With a partner, write a 'seasonal story' (*150 words*) which could only take place in winter, summer, spring or autumn. Before you begin, brainstorm the vocabulary of the season you choose.

30 Roots

Intermediate/Advanced

Gillian Porter Ladousse

Target group: *Young adult / Adult in mono-lingual or multi-lingual classes*

Type of activity: *Listening / Speaking / Cultural awareness*

This is an activity in which the students explore their own cultural origins. Make sure that the students understand that the activity is about the cultural identity (not personal identity) of the group or groups they belong to.

The students listen to questions on topics which have probably shaped their cultural identity. They make brief notes and then compare them. In a multilingual class, the students describe their own cultural origins to each other. In a mono-lingual class, they discuss, agree and disagree about what is important in their impressions of their cultural identity.

Method

1 Copy the handout on page 66–7 – one copy for each student.

2 With an intermediate group, you may need to brainstorm vocabulary on the various topics. In this case, you can begin the activity in one lesson and finish it in another.

3 You can read the script on page 68 to your students, or invent a similar one. It is important to speak in a mellifluous way, keeping a gentle rhythm as if you were doing a guided fantasy, so that you stimulate your learners' imagination. Make sure you allow time for the students to write down their notes.

4 Depending on the time available, you can do one or two sections or the whole activity. The listening and note-taking shouldn't take more than a third of the time available, so that you leave plenty of time for discussion.

5 With an intermediate class, you may like to stop after each section and ask the students to compare notes. With an advanced class, you will probably do the whole listening activity at one go, and then have the discussion.

6 After the students have listened and made notes, they compare their notes. In a monolingual group, make sure they explain to each other how they think the things they have noted down have influenced their cultural identity.

Follow-up

1 The students may like to make some kind of visual record of their findings, such as a map, a diagram, a mind map, or a picture.

2 Ask the students to think of what they would miss most if or when they go abroad. They compare and discuss their choices, giving reasons.

3 Ask the students to write to someone they know or might know who is going to visit their country. They explain what it is essential for a visitor to know about their country. *(150 words)*

31 Find the nine questions

Upper intermediate/Advanced

Jane Revell

Target group: *Young adult / Adult*

Type of activity: *Listening / Question formation*

This activity takes a well-tried EFL technique and turns it into a wonderful surprise – the questions turn out to be the lyrics of a famous Elvis Presley song. For this to work, you will need a cassette with 'Are you lonesome tonight?' by Elvis Presley.

NOTE: It is important that you keep the song a closely guarded secret right up to the very last minute. Talk about a 'text' rather than a song.

Method

1 Tell the students that they are going to practise forming questions. They can work individually or in pairs.

2 Make copies of the handout on page 69 – one copy for each student/pair. Ask them to suggest possible questions to fit. Tell them that they can work on the questions in any order and to write down their ideas.

3 Set a time-limit and check orally with the whole class. Several questions are possible in every case. Accept all of those which are but **don't** tell them if they really hit the nail on the head!

4 Tell the students you are going to play them the text so they can check with the original version.

5 Play the first verse of 'Are you lonesome tonight?' (They will laugh!).

6 Ask them to reconstruct this part of the song using the questions to help them.

7 The students listen again and double-check.

Key

Are you lonesome tonight?

Do you miss me tonight?

Are you sorry we drifted apart?

Does your memory stray to a bright summer day when I kissed you and called you sweetheart?

Do the chairs in your parlour seem empty and bare?

Do you gaze at your doorstep and picture me there?

Is your heart filled with pain?

Shall I come back again?

Tell me dear, are you lonesome tonight?

NOTE: You could of course go on to exploit the second part of the song as well. Bearing in mind the danger of overexposing – and killing – a lovely text, however, I would be inclined to let them listen to it and enjoy it. Finally, if a copy of the song is not available, you could always try singing it yourself!

32 Making similes

Lower Intermediate/Intermediate/Advanced

Jane Revell

Target group: *Young adult / Adult*

Type of activity: *Vocabulary / Quick thinking / Thinking about things in new ways*

This is a group game to challenge students both linguistically and imaginatively.

Method

1 Make copies of one of the handouts on pages 70–2 one copy for each student. The handout you choose will depend on the level of the group (see below). Check that the students are familiar with all the vocabulary.

2 Divide the class into groups of three (with one or two groups of four if necessary), and explain how the game works:

- Student A chooses any word from column X and says it.
- Student B chooses any word from column Y and says 'is like ...' (plus their chosen word).
- Student C says 'because ...' and quickly thinks of a reason! (and gets a point).

If C cannot think of anything, A is allowed to make a suggestion (and get a point). If A is unable to come up with a link, B can have a go (and get the point).

- Student B now begins the next round ...

3 Students play the game for 10 minutes, keeping their own scores.

(Handout 1 on page 70 is for Lower Intermediate students, handout 2 on page 71 for Intermediate students and handout 3 on page 72 for Advanced students.)

Feedback

1 Each group shares their favourite simile with the rest of the class.

2 Ask groups if there were any combinations they had trouble with and get the whole class to think about them.

3 Were there any HUGE winners in any of the groups?

Variations

1 Instead of allowing the second person to hear the first person's word before choosing theirs, you might ask them to write down their choices secretly and simultaneously.

2 Let students go beyond the handout and suggest their own words.

Follow-up

Groups choose any one of the similes they came up with and create and write a story to illustrate it.

Acknowledgement: This idea is a variation on an activity I first encountered in a workshop on the uses of simile and story-telling in Neuro-Linguistic Programming run by Lara Ewing.

33 Sentences from tales

Intermediate/Advanced

Mario Rinvolucri, Pilgrims

Target group: *Young adult / Adult*

Type of activity: *Reading / Writing*

This is a matching pairs exercise based on sentences from fairy tales.

Method

1 Copy and cut out the handout on page 73 – one set for each pair.

2 Ask each pair to match the two halves of the formulaic sentences from fairy tales.

3 Ask one pair to read out their matchings to check that all the students have done their matching correctly.

4 Now, working individually, ask the students to try and create mismatches like:

Mirror, mirror on the wall ... what big eyes you've got!

5 Ask them to take one of their mismatches and write the story for which it is the title.

6 Ask the students to stick their new tales up round the walls of the room so they can read each other's.

Key (correctly matched)

1 – d; 2 – c; 3 – a; 4 – g; 5 – h; 6 – j; 7 – b; 8 – k; 9–e; 10 – i; 11 – f

Acknowledgement: An excellent workshop in Seville in 1995 by Audrey Rajal got me thinking about the creative power of mismatching sentence halves. She presented us with the idea of matching them.

34 Remembering

Intermediate/Advanced

Mario Rinvolucri

Target group: *Young adult / Adult*

Type of activity: *Taking dictation / Discussion*

Method

1 Copy the handout on page 74 – one copy per three students.

2 Dictate the handout to your class (working individually) and ask them to think about their answers to the questions as they write. (Some people love doing two things simultaneously!)

3 When you have dictated the eight questions, ask the students to cover the top part of the questionnaire they have been taking down. Ask them if they can remember the first two questions in the dictation. Find out how they recalled them, or tried to recall them.

4 Now give out the handout so the students, working in threes, can correct any errors in their dictation.

5 Still working in threes ask them to answer each question.

6 Round the lesson off with a whole group discussion about what they have learnt about themselves and others.

Acknowledgement: The thinking in the questionnaire would never have entered my head without the work of Bandler and Grinder in Neuro-linguistic Programming (*The Structure of Magic, vols I and II*) and that of Oliver Sachs (*An Anthropologist from Mars*).

35 The wonderful worldwide names quiz

Elementary

Derek Strange

Target group: *Secondary / Young adult*

Type of activity: *Reading / Vocabulary*

This is a general knowledge and vocabulary quiz for individuals or pairs of students.

Method

1 Copy the handout on page 75 – one copy for each student or pair.

2 Students (individually or in pairs) work through the quiz as quickly as possible, racing against each other to complete it. Set a time-limit of either 10 or 15 minutes. Tell them they can use their dictionaries to look up any vocabulary they do not know, but this will obviously slow them down.

3 Allow all the students time to finish the quiz after the first student/pair has won the race. The students who finish first can go back and try to add more names beginning with the same letters to their answers as they may be able to think of several answers for each question.

4 Check the answers with the whole class.

Key (some suggestions)

Atlantic / Arctic, biscuit / bread / beans, Canada / Chile, door / drainpipe / dining-room, Everest / Eiger, Friday, German, Honda, Iowa / Illinois, June / July, knee, librarian / lumberjack, Mediterranean,

Neptune, orange, pig, Queensland, rose, suit / shirt / sock, turkey, United Nations, Vancouver, whisky / wine, xylophone, yellow, Zambia / Zimbabwe

36 Solve a problem *Lower intermediate*

Derek Strange

Target group: *Secondary / Young adult*

Type of activity: *Reading / Logical deduction*

This is a problem solving activity for individuals, practising comparative and superlative adjectives.

Method

1 Copy the handout on page 76 – one copy for each student.

2 Pre-teach the word surname, if necessary (= family name).

3 The students read the information, the problem and the clues. They then try to solve the problem. They are not allowed to consult with each other.

4 Set a time-limit. While the students are working on the problem draw a blank copy of the grid on the board.

5 At the end of the time, ask students to compare their solutions in pairs for a minute or two.

6 Finally, work through the problem with the whole class, putting ticks in the boxes to show the correct solutions. Ask individual students to read out the completed sentences, to check the answers fully.

Key

	Bell	Carter	Davis	Edwards	160 cms	170 cms	175 cms	180 cms
Alison	√				√			
Anne				√				√
Angela		√					√	
Abbie			√			√		

1 *Ms Alison Bell is 160 centimetres tall.*

2 *Ms Anne Edwards is 180 centimetres tall.*

3 *Ms Angela Carter is 175 centimetres tall.*

4 *Ms Abbie Davis is 170 centimetres tall.*

Acknowledgement: This logical reading puzzle is modelled on puzzles described by Ann Ward in her work with secondary students in Malaysia.

37 Conversation on a train *Lower intermediate and above*

Michael Swan and Catherine Walter

Target group: *Young adult / Adult*

Type of activity: *Fluency practice / Role-play*

This is a group activity for 6–8 students.

Method

1 Divide the class into groups of 6–8. Not all of the class need be in the groups at the beginning. Some can 'join' the train at a later stage. Others can play the parts of ticket inspectors, passport control officers, people selling drinks and sandwiches, etc.

2 Give each person a copy of the handout on page 77 and allow them time to prepare.

3 Arrange the seats in rows of three or four, facing each other. When everyone is ready, they can begin.

Follow-up

1 One of the groups can 'perform' their role-play in front of the others.

2 They can be asked to write a scene – a conversation between two people on the train (15–20 lines). This can be based on what they remember from the role-play.

38 Strange presents *Lower intermediate and above*

Michael Swan and Catherine Walter

Target group: *Young adult / Adult*

Type of activity: *Fluency practice*

This is a group activity based on giving reasons why certain 'unusual' presents would be suitable for you.

Method

1 Copy and cut out the handout on page 78 – one set of 'present' cards for each group.

2 Arrange the students into groups of 6–8. Each group gets a set of cards and places them face down on the table. Each person chooses a card and has 1 minute in which to think about why this 'present' is really suitable for them.

3 They now take it in turns to tell the rest of the group why the 'present' they have been given is so suitable.

4 Set a time-limit. When everyone has finished, ask one or two students, at random, to tell the whole class why their present was so suitable. Alternatively, ask each group to nominate one person from their group to tell the rest of the class – preferably the person who gave the most convincing reason.

Variation

Working individually, each student writes on three separate pieces of paper the names of three things that would make strange presents (e.g. a baby tiger, a rubber clock, a bottle of melted snow, etc.) Collect the papers and give them out to different people in the class – one item for each student. (Make sure no one receives their own item!) Arrange the students into groups of 6–8. They now take it in turns to tell the rest of the group why the 'present' they have been given would be really suitable for them.

39 One word poems *Intermediate*

Brian Tomlinson

Target group: *Teenagers / Young Adult / Adult*
Type of activity: *Vocabulary / Creative writing*

This is an interpretation and a creative writing activity based on one word poems.

Method

1 Copy the handout on page 79 – one copy for each student.

2 Tell the students that they are going to read some one word poems and that as they read each one they should try to make a picture of what the poem means to them in their heads.

Give them an example first by describing or drawing on the board the picture that you make in your head while reading the poem 'Watermouth'.

3 Give out the handout and tell the students to do exercise 1 individually.

4 Tell the students to form groups and to compare their experiences of the ten poems.

5 Tell the groups to select five words from exercise 1 and to put them together to form a new 5-line poem. They can add extra 'linking' words of their own as well if they like.

e.g.

Nowthen

Eggblack then

Lightblue now

Tickchime then

Drumstill now

Oneword.

You could show this example to any group which was not sure what to do.

6 Ask each group to read out their poem.

Follow-up

1 Tell the groups to make up ten one word poems of their own.

2 Get each group to give their poems to another group and then to combine five of the one word poems they are given to make a new five-line poem (as in 5 above).

3 Get the students to produce neat copies of all the poems they have written and then display them on the walls of the classroom.

4 For homework ask each student to write at least five more one word poems.

40 Associations

Elementary/Intermediate/Advanced

Penny Ur

Target group: *All*
Type of activity: *Vocabulary / Rapid scanning / Grammar (Variation 1)*

This is a vocabulary activity based on forming plausible associations between pairs of words.

Method

1 Copy and cut up one of the handouts on pages 80 – 2. Choose a handout appropriate to the level of the group (see note below). Give each student a copy of sheet A and make sure they understand all the vocabulary on their sheets.

2 Ask them to suggest a (plausible!) sentence that links any two of the words. When a student does this, tell them all to find the words and join them with a line. (If you have the facility, it is useful to project a copy using an OHP and draw in the lines yourself as you conduct this part of the activity.) They can, of course, put the verbs in different tenses or numbers, or make the nouns plural when composing their sentences.

3 Then divide them into groups of 4–5 students, and challenge each group to draw in as many lines as it can in 3 minutes, based on sentences suggested by participants. After 3 minutes stop them and count up the lines. Then give out sheet B at their level, and see if they can break their own previous record.

Variations

1 Limit them to a grammatical structure you have been teaching. For example, the sentence must be a comparison, using comparative adjectives; or it must be something that is going on at the moment, using the Present Continuous, etc.

2 Do the same in writing, as an individual or pair activity. Each student (or pair) has 3 minutes to write as many sentences as they can, and draw in the relevant lines on their sheet. Then pool the results with the whole class.

NOTE: The sheets are graded as follows: 1A /1B (*Elementary*), 2A/2B (*Intermediate*) and 3A/3B (*Advanced*).

41 I sympathize *Elementary/Intermediate*

Penny Ur

Target group: *All*
Type of activity: *Getting to know you / Grammar (question formation)*

This is a getting to know you activity for the whole class.

Method

1 Copy the handout on page 83 – one copy for each student.

2 Tell them to fill in the answers to the questions, expressing their own honest opinions.

3 When they have finished, they get up and ask other students in the class the same questions. When they find someone who feels the same way about any of the questions, they write down that person's name under *Sympathizers*.

Variations

1 When you find someone who feels differently from the way you do, find out why, and get them to explain their opinion.

2 Try to find someone who has at least three choices that are the same as yours.

Follow-up

Find out which options got the most votes and why – a sort of class survey and discussion.

NOTE: For children, cut out and use only the first two items.

42 Lost Property

Elementary/Lower intermediate

Peter Viney

Target group: *Young adult / Adult*

Type of activity: *Role-play with whole class participation*

This is a method for involving everyone in a role-play while emphasising the importance of non-verbal communication. The class activity sheet can be used for any other role-plays where there is a confrontation situation. The grammar has been restricted to the past simple.

Method

1 Copy and cut up the handouts on pages 84 – 5. You will need one copy of the role cards for Students A and B, together with enough copies of the Class Activity sheet for each student to have one. (To save paper, two identical copies of the Class Activity sheet are given.)

2 Select a pair to do the role-play. They should not see each other's cards. Send them out of the room while you explain the activity to the rest of the class. Tell them that the person who has lost property is Student A while the Lost Property clerk is Student B.

3 Have Students A and B role-play standing up, while the class observes. Encourage them to move around. The rest of the class watch closely, trying to think about the points on their Class Activity sheet. (They can make rough notes, if they wish.)

4 When Students A and B have finished the role-play, the rest of the class now fill in their Class Activity sheet.

5 Arrange the class into pairs. They compare their observations and report back to the class. Were the students generally in agreement, or were there a lot of different opinions?

6 Discuss the importance of the non-verbal communication in the role-play. Ask the students for some examples of non-verbal communication (e.g. folded arms, gestures, eye contact, smiles, etc.)

7 Repeat with a further pair, who will now be aware of the observation task.

8 Discuss and compare the role-plays. Did students A and B perform 'better' this time?

Acknowledgement: This activity is based on a general approach to role-play used in Peter Viney and Karen Viney's *Handshake – A Course in Communication* (Oxford University Press).

43 Find the hidden sentences

Lower intermediate and above

Peter Watcyn-Jones

Target group: *Young adult / Adult*

Type of activity: *Grammar (word order) / Reading*

This is a simple jigsaw reading type of activity for pairs or groups of three, where the students have to find eight sentences hidden in a grid.

Method

1 Copy the handout on page 86 – one copy for each pair/group.

2 Explain that they have to find eight hidden sentences and then write them down at the bottom of their handout. To help them the first word of each sentence is given, plus one other word. They can only use a word from an adjacent square, but can move vertically, horizontally or diagonally in any direction. They are **not** allowed to use the same word more than once. Finally, point out that not all the words in the grid will be used.

3 Set a time-limit and check orally.

Key

1 Anne and her sister are twins.

2 French people drink a lot of wine.

3 We usually play tennis on Friday.

4 The capital of Indonesia is Jakarta.

5 I love animals, especially dogs.

6 James gave up smoking two years ago.

7 Do you want to know a secret?

8 He met his wife at a party.

44 Do you get easily confused?

Intermediate and above

Peter Watcyn-Jones

Target group: *Young adult / Adult*

Type of activity: *Reading / Puzzle-solving / Grammar (conditionals)*

This activity for pairs or groups tests the students' ability to read logically.

Method

1 Copy the handout on page 87 – one copy for each pair/group.

2 Explain that they only have 10 minutes in which to complete it.

3 Check orally. To avoid cheating, let the students mark one another's handouts.

4 The pair/group with the highest score wins.

Key

(1 point per correct answer)

1 The letter Z should be crossed out.

2 Draw a cross.

3 26 (6 + 20)

4 OCEAN

5 <u>word</u> should be underlined.

6 65

7 5

8 BANANA. (The capital of Wales is Cardiff. Belfast is the capital of Northern Ireland.)

9 Draw a circle around the word 'circle'. An extra point for underlining the word 'man' in sentence number 10.

10 HELP

11 Write which day it is today.

12 NO MORE.

(maximum score: 13 points)

45 Same word – different meaning

Intermediate/Advanced

Peter Watcyn-Jones

Target group: *Young adult / Adult*

Type of activity: *Vocabulary (homonyms)*

This is a vocabulary game for groups. It concentrates on homonyms – words which look the same but can have several meanings.

Method

1 Copy and cut out the 24 words on page 88 or page 89 – one set for each group. The words on page 88 are for intermediate students and the words on page 89 for upper intermediate/advanced students.

2 Divide the class into groups of 4–6 students. Each group will divide itself into two further groups – A and B. Give each group a pile of cards and place them face down on the table. The groups face each other.

3 Group A starts. One person turns over the top card so it is visible to everyone and the group tries to give two different meanings for the word. Group B listens and either accepts or rejects Group A's answer. If successful, Group A retains the card. If not, it is replaced at the bottom of the pile. Explain that some of the words may be pronounced differently. Also that a word might have one meaning as a verb and a completely different one as a noun or an adjective.

4 Play proceeds in this manner, the groups taking it in turns to explain the words.

5 The group with the largest number of cards at the end is the winner.

6 At the end of the game, find out from the whole class if there were any words that caused problems.

Variation

For advanced groups especially, instead of giving two explanations for the words, you can ask them to make up two sentences to show the different meanings.

Key (possible explanations)

Intermediate words

ash (from a cigarette / a tree); ball (a formal dance / used in soccer); bark (sound a dog makes / outer coating of a tree); bill (at a restaurant, a bird's beak); blind (can't see / a sort of curtain); boil (water on a stove / a sore); book (something you read / reserve); bow (bend the body forward / in someone's hair or shoelace); bridge (over a river / a card game); change (loose money / alter something); chest (part of the body / large container); coach (type of bus / someone in charge of athletes, etc.); date (December 1st / a fruit); fair (light in colour / place of amusement); lean (meat with no fat / bend the body); light (not heavy / a match); match (to make fire / a football match); palm (inside of hand / a tree); sole (part of foot / a fish); spring (a season / water); stamp (for a letter / your foot); train (a means of transport / someone e.g. to sing better); watch (tells you the time / watch television); wave (your hands / at the sea)

Advanced words

admit (say you're wrong / allow to enter); bear (animal / can't bear pain); bolt (for a door / what a horse might do if frightened); charge (price / soldiers charge); conduct (behaviour / lead an orchestra); court (tennis court / place where legal matters are settled); desert (area of sand / abandon someone); draught (current of air / preliminary plan or sketch); faint (lose consciousness / not clear); fan (to cool yourself / a keen follower); fence (around a house / to fence with swords); grave (for dead bodies / serious); hide (keep out of sight / animal's skin); leave (depart / permission to be absent e.g. from army); litter (rubbish / litter of puppies); note (musical note / a short written message); private (not public / type of soldier); rear (bring up young / back end of something); refuse (say no / rubbish); row (line of houses / quarrel); sentence (in grammar / a prison sentence); sound (make a noise / area of water); temple (part of the head / religious building); well (for water / not ill)

46 Explain the words

Intermediate/Upper intermediate/ Advanced

Peter Watcyn-Jones

Target group: *Young adult / Adult*

Type of activity: *Vocabulary (explaining words)*

This is a vocabulary game for groups of 5–6 students.

Method

1 Copy, cut out and shuffle the words on page 90 (*intermediate*) or on page 91 (*upper intermediate / advanced*) – one set for each group. The words are handed to the groups face down.

2 Explain that they take it in turns to pick up a card, then try to explain what the word in *italics* means. The rest of the group listen and decide whether the explanation is satisfactory (majority vote, if necessary!). If so, the person keeps the word. If not, it is placed at the bottom of the pile.

3 The student with the highest number of words wins.

4 When they have finished, go through the words to find out if there were any they didn't really understand.

Acknowledgement: This is an adaptation of an idea in *Vocabulary Games & Activities* by Peter Watcyn-Jones (Penguin Books, 1993).

47 The definition game

Intermediate and above

Peter Watcyn-Jones

Target group: *Young adult / Adult*

Type of activity: *Vocabulary (giving definitions)*

This is a vocabulary game for pairs based on being able to make up suitable definitions for ten words so that the other person can guess what the words are.

Method

1 Copy out the handout on page 92 for Student A and on page 93 for Student B. The students sit facing each other, making sure that they cannot see what is written on each other's papers.

2 Explain the rules, namely that Student A starts by asking Student B to explain the ten missing words on his/her sheet. (They can be taken in any order.) To make it slightly easier, certain letters in the missing words are already given. Student A writes down the answer if (s)he thinks (s)he knows it. DO NOT CHECK YET!

3 Student B now asks Student A to explain the missing words on his/her sheet. Again, the answers are written down.

4 Let them check their answers by comparing handouts.

48 Drawing a snippet *Intermediate/Advanced*

Tessa Woodward

Target group: *Young adult / Adult*

Type of activity: *Drawing / Reading comprehension / Discussion*

This is a pair or group activity where students read a short snippet from a newspaper, then try to draw it.

Method

1 Copy and cut up the handouts on page 94 – Give one of the stories to Student A and another to Student B.

2 Students work alone at first. Let them read their handouts. They can check any words they don't understand using a dictionary or by asking you.

3 Once they have read and understood the situation, they start drawing it. Tell them they don't have to be great artists – simple 'matchstick men' drawings will do. They can also have several drawings if necessary to illustrate the story. They are also allowed to write **one** word to help explain the story.

4 They now work in pairs. They take it in turns to show each other their drawings. The student who has the drawing, tries to work out what the story was by asking his/her partner questions. For example:

Is this a man, here?

Is this a washing machine?

Is he taking electricity from the streetlamp?

What does £75 mean? Is that how much money he saved?

Is this a baby? Has it been run over by the car?

etc.

NOTE: These snippets are only suggestions. You can always find your own, but make sure they have a weird situation that can be easily visualised and drawn.

Variation

As above but this time, the students work in groups of four. (You will need to find two extra stories). Each person gets one of the stories to draw. When they have finished, they take it in turns to show the three other members of the groups their drawing. All three students can now ask questions to try to work out what the original story was.

Extra stories

In April 1992, a mugger attacked a woman in Johannesburg. But she took a gun out and locked him into the boot of her car. Then she drove him to the nearest police station.

A woman driver who had her handbag snatched while she waited at a traffic light chased after the thieves in her car – a white BMW. The thieves dropped the handbag, so she got out of her car to pick it up. As she did so, the thieves stole her BMW instead.

49 Modern myths

Lower intermediate and above

Andrew Wright and Julia Dudas

Target group: *All*

Type of activity: *Listening for gist / Speaking (when retelling the story)*

People are usually ready for a story at any time and stories do not need to take too long to tell. Modern myths are a sure fire winner; they only exist because people want to tell them and hear them. You and the students probably know many of them perhaps without realising it. Here's one for you to tell and for the students to retell. If possible try to learn the story in advance so you can tell it more or less as written in the handout.

Method

1 Copy the handout on page 95 – one copy for each student. But do not hand them out yet!
2 Ask the class to make themselves comfortable. Tell the students you are going to tell them a story but there won't be any comprehension exercises to do afterwards. Tell them that some people say it is a true story but you're not sure.
3 Tell the story – preferably by heart. If not, try to read it as 'naturally' as possible.
4 Ask the students to sit in pairs and try to tell the story to each other so that they can retell to their friends or family at another time.
5 Give the students a copy of the story and suggest that they compare it with their own memory and telling of the story. They can, if they wish, modify their own telling by adding details they (or you!) forgot to include.

50 Soap faces

Elementary

Andrew Wright and Julia Dudas

Target group: *All*

Type of activity: *Speaking / Describing a person*

A page of faces is invaluable! Virtually every language teaching point can be practised with them. Here is an activity you can do with sixteen faces.

Method

1 Copy the handout on page 96 – one copy for each group of four students.
2 Each student must think of one of the faces and write down all the information he or she can imagine about that person. The description can be serious but you might suggest to the students that they can make their ideas as funny and outrageous as they wish.
3 The students take it in turns to read out their description. The other students listen and try to guess which person the description refers to.

Variation

1 Copy the handout on page 96 – one copy for each group of four students.
2 Write on the board a selection of the following sentence starters:

   I like people who …

   I don't like people who …

   I like people whose …

   I don't like people whose …

   I like animals which …

   I don't like animals which …

   I like places where …

   I don't like places where …

   I like stories in which …

   I don't like stories in which …
3 The students choose a face, point to it and then take it in turns to complete each sentence on behalf of their chosen character.

Part Two

Material for photocopying

HONESTLY!

Questions to get you talking.

1 Have you ever got off a bus or train without paying?
2 If you found a purse or wallet in the street, what would you do with it?
3 If you found some money on the floor, would you keep it?
4 Have you ever taken something from a shop without paying for it?
5 Have you ever told a 'white lie'?
6 If you were given too much change in a shop, would you tell the shop assistant?
7 When it is your turn to pay, would you ever try to get out of paying?

Now, answer these questions as honestly as you can.

8 *Your friend arrives wearing a new dress. She is pleased with it, but you think it looks terrible. Would you*

A pretend to like it too? ☐
B tell her it didn't suit her? ☐
C say nothing about it? ☐

9 *You are playing a computer game when you suddenly remember that you have some homework. You don't have enough time to do it. What would you do about it?*

A Copy from a friend and pretend it is your own work. ☐
B Make an excuse to the teacher, e.g. that you were ill, or had to do something for your father. ☐
C Ask if you can hand your homework in late. ☐

10 *Someone compliments you on your beautiful garden. They do not know that you pay a gardener to do it for you. How would you react?*

A Say thank you and accept the compliment. ☐
B Admit that it was not your work but the gardener's. ☐
C Change the subject. ☐

11 *You are in your classroom with another student. He starts to smoke a cigarette, which is against school rules. Seeing a teacher coming, he throws it out of the window, but when the teacher comes in, she can smell the cigarette smoke. She looks round and blames you. What would you do?*

A Tell her that it was not you but the other student. ☐
B Take the blame and say nothing. ☐
C Turn to the other student and wait for him/her to own up. ☐

12 *You decide to go for a long cycle ride, but give up after 10 kilometres because you feel tired. Next day, some friends are talking about how they regularly cycle 30 or 40 kilometres. When they ask you how you got on last night, what would you tell them?*

A Say that you stopped after 10 kilometres because you felt tired. ☐
B Say that you did not measure how far you cycled, but it was probably about 25 or 30 kilometres. ☐
C Say that you couldn't go very far because you had to be back by a certain time. ☐

13 *You pay for some goods at the supermarket, and realise that the shop assistant has given you change for a £50 note, whereas you gave him a £20 pound note. What would you do?*

A Point out his mistake. ☐
B Say nothing and hope he doesn't realise. ☐
C Wait till you get home before deciding what to do about it. ☐

14 *The boss tells you a joke which you do not understand at all. What would you do?*

A Laugh anyway. ☐
B Ask him/her to explain it. ☐
C Remain silent, or change the subject. ☐

15 *You are at a party, and a man you do not know starts to make racist or sexist comments which you find very offensive. What would you do?*

A Try to change the subject. ☐
B Pretend to agree with him. ☐
C Tell him how much you dislike his opinions. ☐

16 *Your partner finds a photograph of another girl / boy on your desk. The person in the photo is someone you met on holiday and flirted with. What would you tell your partner?*

A It's someone I met on holiday. ☐
B It's a cousin of mine. ☐
C I know nothing about the photograph. Someone must have left it there. ☐

HONESTLY! Key

How did I do?

8 A This is the most tactful thing to do. *(3 points)*
B Although you are telling the truth, you are not being very *sensitive*. *(2 points)*
C This is the coward's way. *(1 point)*

9 A This is just plain dishonest. *(1 point)*
B Although not completely honest, it is what most people do, so you get 3 points for honestly answering the question! *(3 points)*
C This is noble and deserves 2 points. *(2 points)*

10 A This is what most people would do, so you get 3 points for honestly answering the question! *(3 points)*
B This is honest and deserves 2 points. *(2 points)*
C This is the coward's way. *(1 point)*

11 A Would you really do this? *(1 point)*
B Although this is the *noble* thing to do, it rarely happens. *(2 points)*
C This is the likeliest response in real life. *(3 points)*

12 A This is the plain truth and hurts nobody, not even yourself. *(3 points)*
B This is really naughty. *(1 point)*
C Well, it is a sort of half-truth. *(2 points)*

13 A This is what most people in fact do, despite a momentary temptation. *(3 points)*
B Just plain dishonest. *(1 point)*
C You are probably deceiving yourself, but maybe you are *sincere*. *(2 points)*

14 A Let's face it, it is a small deception to keep your boss happy. *(3 points)*
B Would you really put your job at risk for such an unimportant thing? *(2 points)*
C It might work, but you really ought to take some positive action. *(1 point)*

15 A This is the coward's way. *(2 points)*
B This is both dishonest and cowardly. *(1 point)*
C Well, we all like to think that this is what we would do. *(3 points)*

16 A Well, it is *honest*, but a bit *dangerous*. *(2 points)*
B This is what most people would do, so you get 3 points for honestly answering the question! *(3 points)*
C The coward's way out. *(1 point)*

22–28	You are a person of such high moral character that you must be very difficult to live with. We can only hope that you were not being totally honest when you completed the questionnaire!
15–21	You are a good citizen and a good friend, tempering honesty with tact.
8–14	You are no better and no worse than the rest of us – you mean to be honest, but sometimes you find it hard. And sometimes, you give in to temptation. At least you gave honest answers, didn't you?
0–7	Come on! Either you worry too much about what *other people think of you*, or you didn't answer the questions honestly!

2 MY WORD!

Jake Allsop

PURPLE	3	DESTROY	3	COMPUTER	1
UNHAPPY	2	PREVENT	3	BUS DRIVER	2
SQUARE	3	ENJOY	1	KETTLE	3
SEVENTY-FIVE	2	DROP	2	SWAN	2
PRETTY	1	SNOOZE	3	FILM STAR	1
PLASTIC	2	PREFER	2	QUEEN	2
NOISY	2	STAMMER	3	FOOTBALL PITCH	3
EXPENSIVE	1	SWIM	1	SHIRT	1
STRIPED	3	FORGET	1	CAMEL	2
UGLY	1	WHISTLE	3	FRYING PAN	3
INDEPENDENT	3	SHOW	1	FISH	1
HARD-WORKING	3	HIDE	2	OVERCOAT	2
FAT	1	BUILD	1	BRIDGE	2
JAPANESE	2	SNEEZE	3	CAVE	3
PREHISTORIC	3	MISS	2	GLASSES	1
FLAT	2	SMASH	2	DETECTIVE	2
MAD	1	EXPLAIN	2	BUCKET	2
OPEN	1	APOLOGIZE	3	MONSTER	1
CRUEL	2	KICK	1	GRAND PIANO	3
ACCIDENTAL	3	SMELL	2	VIOLINIST	2
EXTRAORDINARY	2	TAKE AFTER	2	KEY	1
FINAL	3	SCREAM	1	WHEEL	1
PINK	2	CHASE	3	TELESCOPE	2
SCIENTIFIC	2	PUT UP WITH	3	PUDDING	3
SOUR	1	LONG FOR	3	ACROBAT	3
MUSICAL	3	REGRET	2	CHIMNEY	2
GREEDY	1	FONDLE	3	WATERFALL	3
MUSCULAR	3	INVESTIGATE	3	BOTTLE OPENER	2
NORTHERN	2	GIGGLE	2	VOLCANO	2

3 TELLING A STORY

Jan Bell and Roger Gower

1 You are on your way to have an interview for a very important job but the lift stops between floors. There is no emergency button but there is a small hole in the top of the lift. How do you get to the interview on time?

2 You are giving a dinner party for some very important guests in the top floor flat of a very high building. You are having drinks in the room next door and you go into the dining-room to check that everything is ready. Unfortunately, you see a dead body under the table! There is no other door in the room. How do you get the body out without the guests knowing?

3 An old man has lost the secret of his childhood. He wanders all over the world trying to find it but without success. One day he comes across a huge river. There is a forest on the other side and he is sure that he can find the secret of his childhood there. But the river is very deep. He has no boat, he can't swim and there are no rocks in the river. How does he get across?

4 You wanted to parachute into a field. You have jumped from the plane but your parachute hasn't opened. You are falling very fast on to a motorway. There are many cars and lorries below you. You only have the three objects you have chosen to help you. How do you land safely?

5 You are living in a town by the sea. You see somebody rob a bank and run away with the money. You chase the robber through the town and on to the beach. The robber can run faster than you. There is no boat. How do you stop the robber and get the money back?

4 READING DIFFERENT WORLDS

Ron Carter

Text A

1 **Lift handset**
Listen for dial tone. (Continuous purring or new dial tone – high-pitched hum.)

2 **Insert money**
At least minimum fee. Credit display stops flashing on insertion of minimum fee.
Do not insert money for operators of SOS-Emergency (999) calls.
If dial tone stops before you start to dial, press blue follow-on call button, listen for dial tone, then dial number.

3 **Dial number**
Listen for ringing tone. Speak when connected.

Failed call? New call with remaining credit?
Do not replace handset. Press blue follow-on button for dial tone, then re-dial. (Minimum fee still applies. Insert more money, if necessary.)

To continue a dialled call – when you see the display flashing and hear paytone (rapid pips), or any time during call, insert more money.

4 **Replace handset**
Value showing on credit display is not always returnable. Only wholly unused coins returned.

Text B

'A MARTIAN SENDS A POSTCARD HOME'

In homes, a haunted apparatus sleeps,
that snores when you pick it up.

If the ghost cries, they carry it
to their lips and soothe it to sleep

with sounds. And yet, they wake it up
deliberately, by tickling with a finger.

Craig Raine

R. Carter and M. N. Long, The Web of Words by permission of Cambridge University Press.

4 READING DIFFERENT WORLDS
Student question sheet

Ron Carter

Answer the following questions.

1 There are many imperatives in telephone text A, e.g. *lift, insert, dial, replace, listen*, etc. Why? ______

2 Text A also makes use of different kinds of print styles and sizes. Why? ______

3 Why are there so many different paragraphs? What does the layout of the text contribute to the way we read it? ______

4 Now give some thought to how the lines are arranged in text B. Notice, for example, that the line regularly breaks with a verb or verb phrase and that the next line resumes with an adverb or adverbial phrase, e.g. *to their lips, with sounds, deliberately*, etc. What is the effect of the line break upon the reader? ______

5 List all the words in the extract from the poem which are connected with sleep. Why is sleep a dominant image for the view of the telephone given by the 'Martian'? Is it a good comparison? ______

6 Who is the 'they' in the third and fifth lines? ______

7 What is the point of the title of this poem: 'A Martian Sends a Postcard Home'? ______

4 READING DIFFERENT WORLDS
Writing activity

Ron Carter

The poem in text B and others from the volume (from which this is the title poem) give a view of the world of everyday human objects and actions through the eyes of a complete stranger from another planet. Imagine you are a Martian. Write home short 'postcard' descriptions in either poetry or prose of two of the following:

- a television
- a radio
- trying to start the engine of a very old car
- people in a swimming pool
- two people greeting each other. Take one example from your own culture and then one from another culture you know of.
- opening and drinking a bottle or can of Coca-Cola

Poem/Text 1

Poem/Text 2

5 CARDVERSATIONS

Julian Edge

Choose a topic and take it in turns to use the following expressions.

OPEN The first thing is that...	I think that...
But take the example of...	I agree, because...
I disagree, because...	The main point is that...
Maybe, but I still think	Yes, but...
To go back to...	I am quite sure that...
In my experience...	*CLOSE* Can I make one final point?

6 INSERTING WORDS

Simon Greenall

1 Decide where these words go in the passage.

police fluently small heavy bus already

In 1977 Mr Nicholas Scotti of San Francisco decided to visit his relatives in Rome. During the flight, the plane stopped for fuel in New York. Because he hadn't visited Italy since he was a child, he thought he had arrived in Rome.

His nephews weren't there to meet him, but he thought they were delayed by the Roman traffic. He needed to find his way to the station, so he asked a policeman in Italian. By chance the policeman came from Naples and replied in Italian.

When the New York police finally understood what had happened and explained where he was, he refused to believe them. As they were taking him to the airport in a car with its sirens screaming he said,

'Look, I know I'm in Italy. That's how they drive!'

2 Check your answers in pairs.

3 Look at another passage (your teacher will tell you which one) and invent five or six words which can go into it. Make sure the word order is correct. Write the words in random order on a separate sheet of paper.

4 Give your sheet of paper with the words on to your partner. If (s)he can find a position for each word which is different from the position you thought of, (s)he gets a point. If (s)he can only find the position you thought of, you get a point.
Do the same with his/her words.

The person with the highest number of points is the winner.

7 DELETING WORDS

Simon Greenall

1 *Read the passage below and cross out any words which are unnecessary. You cannot cross out two or more words together.*

On a flight across America in 1976, a man rose from his seat, took out a hand gun and pointed it at the air hostess.

'Take me immediately to Detroit,' he said quietly.

'We're already going to Detroit,' she replied calmly.

'Oh . . . good,' he said and sat down again.

2 *Look at a new passage (your teacher will tell you which one) and look for words which are 'unnecessary'. Remember that you cannot cross out two or more words together.*

8 PREDICTING FROM CHECK QUESTIONS (1)

Simon Greenall

Here are some questions about a passage called 'A weekend to remember'. *Read the questions and write full answers to them. Leave a blank if you cannot guess the answer. The first two have been done for you.*

A weekend to remember

1 Where did Marie Jones go for the weekend?
Answer: To visit friends in Wales.

2 What did she take with her?
Answer: Her new ________________.

3 Why did she take it with her?

____

4 What did she do when she got home?

____

5 What did she pick up the following day?

____

6 What was she looking forward to seeing?

____

7 Who did she expect to see in her photos?

____

8 To her surprise, what did she find?

____

9 What did the twenty-four identical photos show?

____

10 What did she think the photographer's shop had done with her photos?

____

11 Who did she complain to the following morning?

____

12 What did she get back from the shop later that day?

____

13 What did the manager explain she had done with the camera?

____

14 What had she taken twenty-four photos of?

____

8 PREDICTING FROM CHECK QUESTIONS (2)

Simon Greenall

Now read the passage and fill in the blanks you left in handout 1.

Marie Jones went to stay with friends in Wales for the weekend. She took her new camera with her to take photos. The weather was beautiful and she took photos of the countryside, her friend's house, her friends, their children and even their pet dog, Bruno.

When she got back home, she went to a local photographer's to get the film developed. The shop assistant told her they would be ready the following day.

She picked the photos up on her way home from work. As soon as she reached her flat, she sat down and opened the packet. She was really looking forward to seeing the photos she had taken. She couldn't believe it when all twenty-four photos showed something light brown and completely out of focus. The shop must have mixed her photos up with someone else's, she thought.

The following morning, on her way to work, she called at the photographer's and complained angrily to the manager about the mix-up. She left the photos with him and he said he would look into it. She agreed to call back on her way home from work.

At 5.30, she turned up at the photographer's, once again looking forward to seeing the 'proper' photos this time. To her surprise, the manager handed back the same photos as before, explaining that she had not held the camera properly. She had taken twenty-four photos of her own right cheek!

9 MEDALS

Jill Hadfield

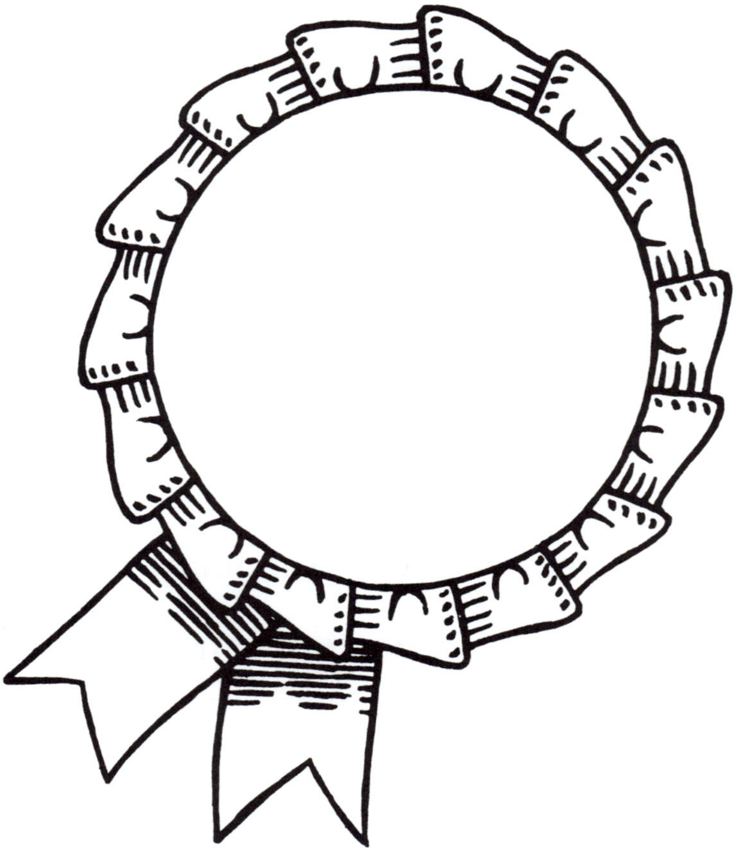

10 REMEMBER WHEN...

Jill Hadfield

Remember when
Remember when
Remember when
Remember when
Remember when
Remember when
Remember when
Remember when
Remember when
Remember when
Remember when
Remember when
Remember when
Remember when
Remember when
Remember when
Remember when
Remember when
Remember when
Remember when

11 MUSICAL STORIES

Jeremy Harmer

Read the sentence in the box and then continue the story. Let the music tell you what to write.

He turned and looked at her.

Now turn the page upside down!

He turned and looked at her.

Read the sentence in the box and then continue the story. Let the music tell you what to write.

12 YOU

Jeremy Harmer

Complete the following.

(a kind of food)	**You**	______________________
(a kind of weather)	**You**	______________________
(a type of furniture)	**You**	______________________
(a means of transport)	**You**	______________________
(an article of clothing)	**You**	______________________
(a part of the house)	**You**	______________________
(a colour)	**You**	______________________
(a month of the year)	**You**	______________________

13 NUMBERS QUIZ

Deirdre Howard-Williams

Look at these expressions with numbers. Can you work out what they mean?

Example

7 D in a W = 7 days in a week

1	12 M in a Y	=	______________________
2	52 W in a Y	=	______________________
3	26 L in the A	=	______________________
4	24 H in a D	=	______________________
5	100 P in a P	=	______________________
6	30 D in S	=	______________________
7	60 S in a M	=	______________________
8	100 Y in a C	=	______________________
9	10 Y in a D	=	______________________
10	4 S in a Y	=	______________________

When you've finished, try these harder ones:

11	The 5 S	=	______________________
12	10 D S	=	______________________
13	12 S of the Z	=	______________________

Now see if you can invent two of your own:

14 ______________________________

15 ______________________________

14 WISH YOU WERE HERE

Deirdre Howard-Williams

Hi there!

I'm having a GREAT time here.

Every day we go ________________ and in

the evening we do a lot of ________________.

The food is delicious, especially ______________.

The only thing I don't like is ________________

and I'm looking forward to

seeing ________________ again.

Wish you were here!

P.S.

15 THE CHICKEN LICKEN STORY

Annie Hughes

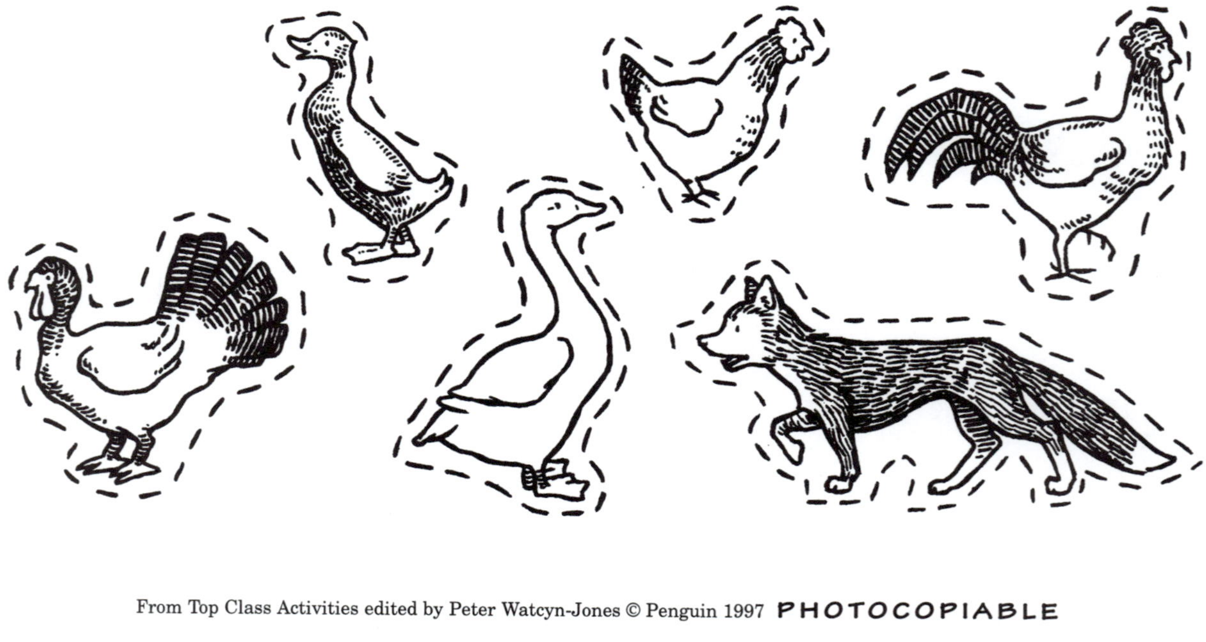

15 THE CHICKEN LICKEN STORY
Teacher's sheet

Annie Hughes

Read the following story to your class.

One day a little chick, chicken licken, was walking through the wood when 'plop' an acorn fell on his head.

'Oh!' said chicken licken 'The sky is falling down. I must go and tell the king.' So, off he went, down the road to tell the king.

On the way he met a hen – 'henny penny'.

'Oh, hello chicken licken,' said henny penny. 'How are you today?'

'I'm fine thanks, but the sky is falling and I am going to tell the king.'

'Then I'll go with you,' said henny penny. So chicken licken and henny penny went off down the road to tell the king.

On the way they met a duck – 'ducky lucky'.

'Oh, hello chicken licken, henny penny,' said ducky lucky. 'How are you today?'

'We're fine thanks, but the sky is falling and we are going to tell the king.'

'Then I'll go with you,' said ducky lucky. So chicken licken, henny penny and ducky lucky went off down the road to tell the king.

On the way they met a goose – 'goosey loosey'.

'Oh, hello chicken licken, henny penny, ducky lucky,' said goosey loosey. 'How are you today?'

'We're fine thanks, but the sky is falling and we are going to tell the king.'

'Then I'll go with you,' said goosey loosey. So chicken licken, henny penny, ducky lucky and goosey loosey went off down the road to tell the king.

On the way they met a turkey – 'turkey lurkey'.

'Oh, hello chicken licken, henny penny, ducky lucky, and goosey loosey,' said turkey lurkey. 'How are you today?'

'We're fine thanks, but the sky is falling and we are going to tell the king.'

'Then I'll go with you,' said turkey lurkey. So chicken licken, henny penny, ducky lucky, goosey loosey and turkey lurkey went off down the road to tell the king.

On the way they met a cockerel – 'cocky locky'.

'Oh, hello chicken licken, henny penny, ducky lucky, goosey loosey and turkey lurkey,' said cocky locky. 'How are you today?'

'We're fine thanks, but the sky is falling and we are going to tell the king.'

'Then I'll go with you,' said cocky locky. So chicken licken, henny penny, ducky lucky, goosey loosey, turkey lurkey and cocky locky went off down the road to tell the king.

On the way they met a fox – 'foxy loxy'.

'Oh, hello chicken licken, henny penny, ducky lucky, goosey loosey, turkey lurkey and cocky locky,' said foxy loxy. 'How are you today?'

'We're fine thanks, but the sky is falling and we are going to tell the king.'

'Follow me,' said foxy loxy. So chicken licken, henny penny, ducky lucky, goosey loosey, turkey lurkey, and cocky locky followed foxy loxy.

They went down the road, over a bridge, past a field, and into a wood. They came to a big hole.

'This is where the king lives,' said foxy loxy. 'Follow me.'

Into the hole went chicken licken, into the hole went henny penny, into the hole went ducky lucky, into the hole went goosey loosey, into the hole went turkey lurkey, into the hole went cocky locky. That night foxy loxy, Mrs foxy loxy and all the little foxy loxies had a delicious supper!

16 IT'S WRITTEN IN THE STARS (1)

Annie Hughes

Complete the following using the personality profile chart.

1 My good points are that I am ________________ and ________________.

(Choose two from Section 1 in the personality profile chart.)

2 My bad points are that I am ________________ and ________________.

(Choose two from Section 2 in the personality profile chart.)

3 In appearance I ________________________________

____

____

(Choose words from Section 3 in the personality profile chart.)

4 I never have problems with my health. _____ *(tick (√) if correct)*

or I sometimes have a problem with/suffer from ________________

____

____

(Choose from Section 4 in the personality profile chart.)

5 Three jobs that would suit me would be the following:

(a) ________________

(b) ________________

(c) ________________

(Choose three from Section 5 in the personality profile chart.)

6 I like ________________ and ________________.

(Choose two from Section 6 in the personality profile chart.)

7 I don't like ________________ or________________.

(Choose two from Section 7 in the personality profile chart.)

When you have finished, pass your paper to your partner.

16 IT'S WRITTEN IN THE STARS (2)

PERSONALITY PROFILE CHART

Annie Hughes

Section 1: Personality (good points)

caring
cautious
charming
co-operative
creative
dependable
energetic
entertaining
enthusiastic
hard-working
honest
kind
loving
loyal
optimistic
protective
sensitive
sympathetic
versatile
very loving
witty

Section 2: Personality (bad points)

a gambler at heart
anxious
big-headed
easily embarrassed
flirtatious
hot-headed
impatient
indecisive
irritable
jealous
moody
must be the boss
nervous
not very honest
possessive
quickly bored
rude
self-interested
self-pitying
stubborn
temperamental
too easily hurt
unforgiving
untidy

Section 3: Appearance

I have...
a beautiful complexion
a beautiful smile
a broad face
a high forehead
intense eyes
large eyebrows
large feet
an oval face with large eyes
a rather long neck
small eyes which are far apart
sparkling eyes
a straight nose

I am...
overweight
rather short
serious-looking
slim
taller than average

Section 4: Possible health problems

ankles
asthma
back
circulation
digestive system
eating disorders
eyes
feet
head
heart
hips
kidneys
knees
legs
lungs
nerves
nose
skin
stomach
throat

Section 5: Suitable jobs

actor
artist
baker
banker
beautician
business person
civil servant
detective
engineer
farmer
journalist
mechanic
nurse
photographer
politician
scientist
secretary
soldier
solicitor
surgeon
teacher
vet
writer

Section 6: Likes

being among people
being fussed over
children and pets
collecting things
comfort
friends
gambling
gardening
having strange friends
home and family
making lists
new clothes
parties
peace and quiet
poetry
privacy
punctuality
romantic places
shopping trips
sport
surprises
talking
travelling
winning

Section 7: Dislikes

any criticism of my home
being asked personal questions
being ignored
being kept waiting
being laughed at
being second
being told to hurry up
change
crowds and noise
loud arguments
making mistakes
making promises
new things and ideas
noisy, crowded places
people who show off
sharing
sitting still for a long time
ugly places
unhappy friends
untidiness
violence and fighting
waiting for things

16 IT'S WRITTEN IN THE STARS (3)

HOROSCOPE CHART

Annie Hughes

Zodiac Sign	Personality Good points	Personality Bad points	Appearance	Health problems	Typical job	You like	You dislike
Aries 22 March–20 April	energetic enthusiastic	jealous must be the boss	rather long neck	eyes head	politician surgeon	new clothes sport	waiting for things!
Taurus 21 April–21 May	dependable very loving	stubborn easily embarrassed	beautiful complexion large feet	throat	farmer business person	comfort gardening	change being told to hurry up
Gemini 22 May–22 June	entertaining and charming versatile	quickly bored impatient	slim	lungs	journalist artist	talking being among people	being laughed at being kept waiting
Cancer 23 June–23 July	kind sensitive	too easily hurt possessive	eyes small and far apart	stomach eating disorders	baker nurse	friends shopping trips	sharing any criticism of your home
Leo 24 July–23 August	brave generous	stubborn big-headed	oval face with large eyes	heart back	solicitor soldier	winning children and pets	unhappy friends being ignored
Virgo 24 August–23 September	witty and charming sympathetic	untidy irritable nervous	high forehead straight nose	nerves digestive system	secretary mechanic	making lists punctuality	crowds and people sitting still for a long time
Libra 24 September–23 October	charming co-operative	indecisive flirtatious	beautiful smile	kidneys back	beautician politician	peace and quiet being fussed over	ugly places loud arguments
Scorpio 24 October–22 November	caring protective	moody jealous	broad face intense eyes	nose throat	scientist detective	winning collecting things	making mistakes being asked personal questions
Sagittarius 23 November–22 December	honest optimistic	hot-headed a gambler at heart	sparkling eyes can be overweight	hips legs asthma	teacher writer vet	travelling gambling parties	waiting making promises
Capricorn 23 December–19 January	hard-working cautious	unforgiving anxious	serious-looking	knees skin	banker civil servant	home and family privacy	new things and ideas untidiness
Aquarius 20 January–19 February	loyal caring	rude self-interested	taller than average	ankles circulation	photographer engineer	surprises having strange friends	violence and fighting people who show off
Pisces 20 February–21 March	loving and caring creative	self-pitying temperamental	usually short large eyebrows	feet	actor writer	poetry romantic places	noisy, crowded places being second

CAN YOU SEE IT? – CAN YOU MAKE IT OUT?

Replace the verbs in italics in the sentences by phrasal verbs from those below. You will not need all the phrasal verbs, but some verbs are worth more than others – and you want to score as many points as you can!

blow up (10)
bring up (15) call off (10) carry out (5) cut off (10)
give up (10) hold up (10) look up (5) make out (15)√
make up (5) put up (10) run down (15) shut up (10)
work out (5)

Example: I can't quite *see it* from here. I can't quite **make it out** from here.

1 Can you *solve* it?

____

2 I don't believe you! You're *inventing it all*!

____

3 The weather was so bad they had to *cancel* the game.

____

4 We're going to be late. We've been *delayed* in heavy traffic.

____

5 That telephone receptionist *interrupted my conversation*!

____

6 My uncle used to smoke, but he has finally *stopped it*.

____

7 Now that he can talk, they just can't *stop him talking*.

____

8 Can you help me *inflate* these balloons?

____

9 He was *raised and educated* in London.

____

10 They often *criticize* him.

____

Your scores: 1 ____ 2 ____ 3 ____ 4 ____ 5 ____
6 ____ 7 ____ 8 ____ 9 ____ 10 ____

TOTAL [ ]

18 HOME!

Roy Kingsbury

In pairs, read and reorder these paragraphs to make a sensible, logical story. The first pair to shout 'Home!' and to get the paragraphs in the correct order wins the game.

A Not surprisingly, and as a direct consequence of waiting, they soon realized that the tide was coming in and that it might be almost impossible to walk across. But they decided at least to try.

B Because they had experienced such a narrow escape, it put them off making another attempt. So they decided to stay on the island overnight.

C The girls were on an adventure camping holiday, and one of their tasks was to cross to the island from the mainland and back again. They had been waiting for days for the water to subside enough for them to walk across to the island some six kilometres out in the channel.

D They had only walked out some 500 metres before the water began to reach to their knees. They looked at each other – and ran back to the island. They could have been drowned!

E On the following morning, the Friday, because the tide was once more very low, they found that they were again able to cross the six kilometres to the mainland without getting more than their feet wet! They were very relieved!

F And it was while they were swimming, off the other side of the island that the tide began to come in again up the channel between the island and the mainland.

G Suddenly, on the Thursday morning, at low tide, they could see mud and sand all the way out. They quickly packed some food and drink and set off. Because it was heavy going, it took them two hours, so they decided to rest, eat and have a swim off the other side of the island before returning.

---

19 NONSENSE!

Roy Kingsbury

Read each sentence below very carefully and decide which column to tick (✓).

- *If the sentence is grammatically correct and makes sense, tick column A.*
- *If the sentence is total nonsense (i.e. if the grammar is all wrong, the word order wrong, etc.), tick column B.*
- *If the sentence is grammatically correct and perhaps sounds strange, but might be 'philosophical', tick column C.*

	Examples	A Sensible	B Nonsense	C Philosophical
	Fish swim.	✓		
	Fish may think effortlessly.			✓
	Darkly fish might be flown.		✓	
1	Men walk fast.			
2	Fast people always walk.			
3	Fast walk men and women do.			
4	Gently giraffes clean.			
5	Sisters are always annoying.			
6	Elephants remember everything.			
7	Bored brother never met she.			
8	Some people may fly at night.			
9	A train thundered by noisily.			
10	Eaten was greedily the blackbird.			
11	Snakes spend hours thinking.			
12	Lions keen of sport rarely are not.			
13	Silently a red jet aircraft wanted.			
14	Pleased of winning we have.			
15	A book is a collection of written thoughts.			

Your score: Sentences

1	5	9	13 ......
2	6	10	14 ......
3	7	11	15 ......
4	8	12	TOTAL

20 WORD ARRAY
Student's sheet

Alan Maley

silence	said	met	most	don't
sent	what	I	but	flowers
never	we	spoke	he	in
took	in	wrote	of	how
me	was	parks	letters	it
restaurants	love	remember	anyway	

1 *Make up at least eight sentences using the words from the above box. You can use a word as many times as you like, but you are not allowed to change it in any way. You do not have to use all the words. Write your sentences here:*

____

____

____

____

____

____

____

____

____

____

____

2 *Now work in groups of three. Compare your lists. Add to your own list if you wish.*

3 *Working as a group, use some of your sentences to write a short text (a story, a poem, etc.).*

4 *Read out your text to the rest of the class.*

20 WORD ARRAY

ORIGINAL TEXT

Alan Maley

Here is the original text, for comparison with your own texts:

He never sent me flowers. He never wrote me letters. He never took me to restaurants. He never spoke of love. We met in parks. I don't remember what he said, but I remember how he said it. Most of it was silence anyway.

Leszek Szkutnik

21 MINING A TEXT

Alan Maley

Text 1

Ken woke from a confused dream. Gradually his eyes focused. The first thing he noticed was a hand a few inches in front of his face. The fingers were like a bird's claw, stiff, blue with cold. With a shock, he realised that the hand belonged to him. At the same time, he became fully aware of just how cold he was. His bones felt like frozen lead. He remembered an incident from the previous day; he had been hanging about near the kitchen entrance of the Strand Palace Hotel, scavenging for scraps, when a delivery van arrived. The driver had carried in whole sides of beef, the red and white meat refrigerated into hard blocks. He now felt like that frozen meat, his back cold and stiff as a corpse.

Text 2

Margaret Jenkins sat on a bench in Hyde Park, keeping a watchful eye on Mandy. The child was chasing the pigeons in the dappled sunlight under the big plane trees. It was spring and the lawns were splashed with clumps of bright yellow daffodils. She thought of her own childhood. There had been daffodils then too, but wild ones in the fields behind the farm. She often found herself remembering things like this these days. What if she had stayed on the farm and never gone to Cambridge, never met Bill, never had Mandy …?

She pushed these disturbing thoughts out of her mind as Mandy shambled towards her across the grass. In her hand the five-year-old child clutched a pigeon's feather. Mandy offered it to her like a precious possession. Her large head lolled to one side and her slack mouth dribbled saliva, as always, but her eyes were bright with pleasure. Margaret took her daughter into her arms. Some people walking by turned to look at them. In their eyes she recognized a mixture of pity and disgust. Never mind, she was used to it now. How could they understand? Mandy slobbered and shrieked with delight.

Text 3

Milmaq was a solitary person. He would spend hours in the forest, not hunting, simply sitting still, watching, waiting for something to happen. A spider would swing its thread across the canyon between two branches. A woodpecker would drum at the trunk of a chestnut tree, its neck a blur of speed. Above all, the trees themselves would speak to him. He would be aware of them creaking and swaying in the wind. He could sense the sap rising in them in the springtime; feel their sorrow at the approach of winter. If he put his ear to the trunk of a tree, he could hear it growing, very slowly; feel it moving towards its final magnificent shape.

(The above texts are taken from *Campbell's Crossing and Other Short Stories* by Alan Maley, published by Penguin Books, 1994.)

22 WELCOME TO RAACH!

Alan McConnell-Duff

Choose at least two quotations for your speech from the following.

Sonnet No. 18

Shall I compare thee to a summer's day?
Thou art more lovely and more temperate
Rough winds do shake the darling buds of May,
And summer's lease hath all too short a date;
Sometime too hot the eye of heaven shines,
And often is his gold complexion dimm'd;
And every fair from fair sometime declines,
By chance, or nature's changing course,
untrimm'd;
But thy eternal summer shall not fade,
Nor lose possession of that fair thou ow'st;
Nor shall Death brag thou wander'st in his shade,
When in eternal lines to time thou grow'st.
So long as men can breathe or eyes can see,
So long lives this, and this gives life to thee.

William Shakespeare

You can write the opening words of the Mayor's speech here:

23 MEAN THE MEANING

John McRae

Read the following text.

It certainly is most wretched weather. At all events, it is so, now, at the time I am writing and if it isn't particularly unpleasant when I come to be read, it soon will be.

It always is wretched weather, according to us. The weather is like the Government, always in the wrong. In summer time we say it is stifling; in winter that it is killing; in spring and autumn we find fault with it for being neither one thing nor the other, and wish it would make up its mind. If it is fine, we say the country is being ruined for want of rain; if it does rain, we pray for fine weather. If December passes without snow, we indignantly demand to know what has become of our good old-fashioned winters, and talk as if we had been cheated out of something we had bought and paid for; and when it does snow, our language is a disgrace to a Christian nation. We shall never be content until each man makes his own weather, and keeps it to himself.

If that cannot be arranged, we would rather do without it altogether.

Taken from: *Idle Thoughts of an Idle Fellow* by Jerome K Jerome

After you have finished reading the text, working in groups, do the following.

1 Make a list of any words or phrases in the text which you didn't know the meaning of.

2 Now discuss which of these you can guess the meaning of from the context. Cross out these words from your list.

3 Now from the words that are left, put them in order of importance under one of the following headings.

Need to know	Would like to know	Don't really need to know

4 Finally, discuss and decide upon just **one** word or phrase that you really need to know.

24 BEN BATTLE

John McRae

Ben Battle was a soldier bold,
And used to war's alarms;
But a cannon-ball took off his legs,
So he laid down his arms.

Thomas Hood

25 WHAT DO YOU DO WITH THIS?

Terry Moston

Here are some unusual English words. Three possible uses are given for each word, but only one is correct. Choose one of the three uses and write it down. When you have finished, compare your answers with the correct definitions. Did you say anything funny?

1 What do you do with a *tureen*?
- a Put it on your head.
- b Put it in your pocket.
- c Put soup in it.

2 What do you do with *varnish*?
- a Feed it to the cat.
- b Clean the floor with it.
- c Paint it on your furniture.

3 What do you do with a *ewe*?
- a Cut it into small pieces.
- b Put it in a field.
- c Give it to your mother.

4 What do you do with a *haggis*?
- a Cook it for lunch.
- b Read it.
- c Feed it.

5 What do you do with *crockery*?
- a Plant a cactus in it.
- b Put it on the table at mealtimes.
- c Hide it before anyone sees it.

6 What do you do with *gruel*?
- a Hang it in your window.
- b Paint it black.
- c Feed it to someone who is ill.

7 What do you do with a *dibble*?
- a Use it in the garden.
- b Immediately report it to the police.
- c Put a stamp on it and post it.

8 What do you do with *kedgeree*?
- a Polish it and show it to your friends.
- b Eat it hot or cold.
- c Make a summer dress out of it.

Follow-up activity

Make your own quiz.

- Find some unusual words in an English-English dictionary. Write out the words and their correct definitions. (You may want to simplify the dictionary definitions.)
- Add two incorrect definitions for each word. Make your definitions believable.
- Quiz a partner, a group or your class on your words. How many people can you get to believe your definitions?

Key

Here are the correct definitions.

tureen A deep bowl with a lid, from which soup is served.
varnish Varnish gives a hard, shiny, transparent coat when painted on to wooden furniture.
ewe A female sheep
haggis A Scottish dish made from the minced heart, lungs, and liver of a sheep or calf, suet and oatmeal, seasoned with salt, pepper, onions, etc., and boiled like a large sausage in the stomach of the animal.
crockery Plates and cups
gruel A light soup (often given to invalids) made by boiling oatmeal in water or milk, sometimes with the addition of other ingredients, such as butter, sugar, spices, onions, etc.
dibble A gardening tool for making holes in the ground for seeds, bulb, or young plants.
kedgeree An Indian dish of rice with lentils, onions, eggs, butter and spices.

26 FUNNY FACE

Terry Moston

Work with a partner. You are going to draw your partner's face. Your partner is going to draw you. Use the egg shape opposite.

Before you start, draw two very thin lines inside the egg. The first line (Line A) goes down the middle of the egg from top to bottom. The second line (Line B) goes from left to right about half-way from the top. The two lines make a cross (+) in the centre.

1 To draw the eyes

Line B is where the eyes will go. Draw the eyes now.

2 To draw the nose

Line A is where the nose will go. Draw on Line A a short line half-way between the eyes and the bottom of the egg. The top of the nose starts between the eyes; the bottom of the nose ends at the mark. Draw the nose now.

3 To draw the ears

The top of the ears starts where the top of the eyes are. The bottom of the ears ends where the bottom of the nose is. Draw the ears now if you can see them under the hair.

4 To draw the mouth

Draw a short line on Line A half-way between the bottom of the nose and the bottom of the egg. This is where the mouth will go. Draw the mouth now.

top

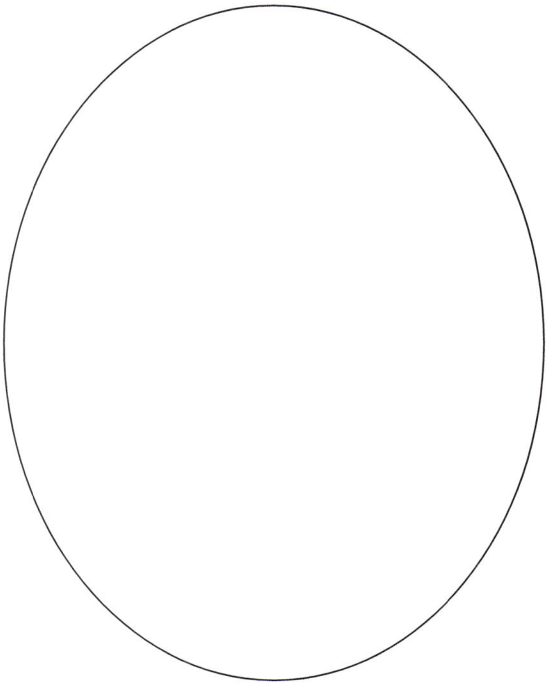

bottom

5 To draw the hair

Some of the hair will be inside the egg. Some of the hair will be outside the egg. Look at your partner carefully. Draw the hair now.

Anything else? Glasses? Earrings? Draw them now.

Now you have finished!

Show your partner your drawing.
Say what you think of your partner's drawing.

The	…	is are really good.	
My	ears eyes	aren't like that. aren't ... enough.	They're too … They should be …
	nose mouth hair	isn't right. isn't … enough.	It's too … It should be …

Opposites

long	short
big	small
wide	narrow
fair	dark
thin	fat
curly	straight

27 A PARALLEL EXERCISE

Robert O'Neill

Talk about the differences between Constance Sunshine and yourself.

> Constance lives in a beautiful and very big house in Southern California. She has three cars, one of which is a Mercedes Benz. She also has a Ferrari as well as a Cadillac Seville, a swimming pool, seven different boyfriends (one for each day of the week) and a small poodle called Rambo.

Here is just one possible answer.

> 'I don't live in a beautiful and big house. I live in a ... and it's in ... I've got just one car. It's a ... I don't want seven different boy/girlfriends. I haven't got any pets, either.'

Now continue with these.

1 Constance loves all animals, particularly poodles.

2 Her favourite food is cold salmon and caviar, which she usually drinks down with champagne.

3 Constance's greatest ambition in life is to stay young and healthy forever.

4 She has four or five holidays a year, and usually spends them in Hawaii.

Now compare yourself with her number one or 'Sunday' boyfriend, Harry Chest.

5 Harry's favourite form of relaxation is lifting weights and wind-surfing.

6 He loves old Elvis Presley records and Country and Western music.

7 He gets up every morning around 5.

8 He usually goes to bed before 10 p.m.

9 One of the things he is very proud of is his collection of tattoos. He has five on his chest, two on each arm and ten more on other parts of his body.

28 WHAT DO YOU THINK IS THE REST OF THE STORY?

Robert O'Neill

These short texts are only fragments of a story. Discuss the questions with someone else. If you can't answer a question, ignore it and find another question you can answer. Above all, remember that there is no one 'correct answer'. There are only many different answers.

1

The woman was well-dressed and in her late twenties. She was sitting at one of the corner tables with an older man. He was talking to her intensely, but in a very low voice.

'No,' she suddenly said.

She threw a glass of wine in his face. Then she jumped up, and ran out of the restaurant. The older man ran after her.

'Jennifer. For God's sake, stop. Try to understand,' he shouted.

It was raining and the street was badly lit. A car had just turned the corner and was coming towards her very fast. The driver probably didn't see her. And she didn't seem to notice the car as she ran out into the middle of the street.

1. What do you think they were talking about? Try to imagine something one or the other actually said.
2. What do you think happened after she ran out into the street?
3. Imagine you happened to pass the restaurant only a few minutes later. Describe what you saw and heard.
4. How do you 'see' either the woman or the man? Try to describe what he or she was wearing, the colour of her or his hair, etc.
5. What do you think are some other 'fragments' of this story – either something that had happened before or later?

2

I had just gone into a big department store in London. I saw a young man in a t-shirt running down the 'up' escalator. He had a bag of some kind in one of his hands. I couldn't really see it very well. The other shoppers tried to get out of his way. He ran past me and out of the door into the street.

Then I saw another man. He came running down the 'up' escalator, too. He was wearing a kind of suit and was about thirty. I watched him as he ran out of the door into the street, too. He stopped for a moment, looked to his right and then to his left. Then he began running again.

1. Why was the young man running?
2. Why was the other man running?
3. Imagine you had gone into the store a few minutes earlier. You saw the young man on one of the other floors just before he started running. Describe everything you saw or that you think happened.
4. Why did the older man stop when he ran out of the door?
5. Why did he begin running again?
6. What happened after that?
7. Describe what the younger man did a few hours later. Where was he? Who spoke to him? What did they actually say?

29 THEY ALWAYS TALK ABOUT THE WEATHER

Gillian Porter Ladousse

THE BEAUFORT WIND SCALE

0 Calm; smoke rises vertically.

1 ______________________________

2 ______________________________

3 ______________________________

4 ______________________________

5 ______________________________

6 ______________________________

7 Whole trees in motion; difficulty walking against the wind.

8 ______________________________

9 ______________________________

10 ______________________________

11 ______________________________

12 Very rarely experienced, accompanied by widespread damage.

29 THEY ALWAYS TALK ABOUT THE WEATHER

Gillian Porter Ladousse

Student A

The Beaufort wind scale is used to describe the wind. It goes from 0 to 12. With your partner, put the descriptions on your cards on the grid in the right order.

a Large branches in motion; telegraph wires whistle, umbrellas used with difficulty.

b Leaves and small twigs in constant motion; light flag blows in the wind.

c Slight structural damage occurs.

d Calm; smoke rises vertically. *0*

e Wind felt on face.

f Breaks twigs off trees; generally makes walking difficult.

g Very rarely experienced; accompanied by widespread damage. *12*

29 THEY ALWAYS TALK ABOUT THE WEATHER

Gillian Porter Ladousse

Student B

The Beaufort wind scale is used to describe the wind. It goes from 0 to 12. With your partner, put the descriptions on your cards on the grid in the right order.

a Whole trees in motion; difficulty walking against the wind. *7*

b Direction of wind shown by smoke but not by wind vanes.

c Trees uprooted; considerable structural damage occurs.

d Whole trees in motion; inconvenience in walking against the wind.

e Devastation occurs.

f Small trees in leaf begin to sway; small crested waves on inland waters.

g Very rarely experienced; accompanied by widespread damage. *12*

30 ROOTS
Student's sheet

Gillian Porter Ladousse

Think about the country or countries where you have roots. Listen to the questions and make brief notes under the following headings. You do not have to answer all the questions.

GEOGRAPHY

size ________________________________

landscape ________________________________

people ________________________________

agriculture ________________________________

industry ________________________________

neighbours ________________________________

GEOLOGY

soil ________________________________

rock ________________________________

PEOPLE ________________________________

size ________________________________

other physical characteristics ________________________________

HISTORY

events ________________________________

heroes and heroines ________________________________

30 ROOTS
Student's sheet (*continued*)

Gillian Porter Ladousse

ART AND CULTURE

myths and legends ______________________________

painters ______________________________

writers ______________________________

musicians ______________________________

other? ______________________________

SOCIETY

political regime ______________________________

families ______________________________

schools ______________________________

standard of living ______________________________

work ______________________________

OTHER PLACES

____

____

____

____

OTHER PEOPLE

____

____

____

____

30 ROOTS
Teacher's sheet

Gillian Porter Ladousse

Read the following to the class.

You are going to think about the culture of the community or the communities that you belong to, and the way this or these cultures have developed.

First, think about the geography.

How big is your country. Is it big or small, or medium size? What's the landscape like? Are there mountains? Is it flat? Are you by the sea? Are there farms, or is it industrial? What else is there? Do you live in an environment which is all the same or which has varied features. What about neighbouring countries?

Now think about the geology.

What kind of soil is there? What about the rock underneath it? How has this affected the people of your country?

What about the people in your country?

How tall are they? Are they dark or fair? Are they the same as the people who live in neighbouring countries?

What about your country's history?

What are the main historical events? Has your history been peaceful, or have there been lots of wars? Name two or three of your national heroes or heroines. How have they affected the history of your country? What achievements are the people in your country proud of?

What about the art and culture in your country?

What are the most important myths and legends of your country? Who are the most important painters, musicians, writers, photographers, sculptors, architects, etc.

Now think about society.

What kind of society do you live in? What kind of political regime? How big are the families in your country? Is there a class system? What kind of education do children have? Are people well-off or is life hard? Do people work long hours, or are they relaxed about their jobs?

Now think about other countries and other people.

Think about aspects of culture of other countries which have influenced your country. Which aspects do you like? Think about people from other countries who are living in your country. What aspects of their culture do you like?

31 FIND THE NINE QUESTIONS

Jane Revell

*Write down **one** question to correspond to each of these answers. (Several questions are possible for each answer.)*

1 ____?

No, I'm not. I like being on my own.

2 ____?

No, I don't. I'm too busy to miss you.

3 ____?

Yes, I'm a little bit sorry, but people do drift apart, don't they?

4 ____?

Yes, it strays to that day sometimes. Not often, though.

5 ____?

No, the chairs seem quite normal.

6 ____?

No, I don't. I'm not a very visual person anyway.

7 ____?

No, it isn't. It's filled with relief.

8 ____?

I wouldn't come back again if I were you!

9 ____?

For the second time – No, I'm not. I like being on my own.

32 MAKING SIMILES (1)
Lower intermediate

Jane Revell

X is like Y because ...

What exciting combinations can you make?

X

a baby
a birthday
a boss
a brother
a child
a dog
fear
a friend
a good film
a grandparent
happiness
home
a husband
love
a man
money
a mother
music
a parent
a politician
peace
school
sport
a teacher
television
a woman
work

Y

an aeroplane	a good film	a park
autumn	a flower	a photograph
a bank	a holiday	a policeman
a belt	a hospital	a radio
a bicycle	a hotel	rain
a boat	an illness	a river
a bottle of wine	January	the sea
a bus	a jug	a ship
a chair	a knife	a shirt
a Chinese restaurant	a lake	a song
chocolate	learning English	a supermarket
a cinema	a market	a telephone
a cloudy sky	a mountain	a train
the colour red	a moustache	a tree
a detective	a museum	the weather
an egg	a newspaper	the weekend
an envelope	the number thirteen	the wind
football	a pair of glasses	winter

A: X ...
B: ... is like Y
C: ... because ...

Example:
A: Love ...
B: ... is like a good film...
C: ... because it's very exciting!
Or: because it can make you cry.
Or: because you want it to go on and on ...
Or: because you don't know what will happen next.
Or: ... etc.

32 MAKING SIMILES (2)
Intermediate

Jane Revell

X is like Y because ...

What exciting combinations can you make?

X

anger
an army
bad advice
beer
a coward
death
an exam
fashion
fear
a fool
a foreigner
freedom
a friend
the future
God
a good meal
happiness
home
hope
intelligence
a kiss
life
love
a man
marriage
music
pain
peace
sport
a teenager
war
a woman
work

Y

an alarm clock
an ambulance
a bad dream
a balloon
a beautiful sunset
blood
a blunt razor
a box of chocolates
a bridge
a bunch of red roses
a burglar
a butcher's shop
a car park
a castle
a chimney
the colour black
a computer
daylight
a dead body
a dentist
a desert
a dripping tap
a duck
an empty glass
an expensive diamond
a dictionary
a film star
fine weather
a flame
a football match
a forest
a fridge
a game of chess
a ghost
good wine
hair
a handbag
a headache
an Indian curry
a joke
a long journey
a jungle
a ladder
learning English
a lift
lightning
a locked door
London
a map
medicine
a motorway
a mouse
yesterday's news
an old sofa
an onion
an operation
an out-of-tune piano
a pair of curtains
a passport photograph
a penguin
a pillow
a pizza
a plastic bag
poison
a postcard
a river
a rotten apple
the Russian alphabet
sex
a snake
a spider
a strawberry
Sunday
a supermarket
a surname
a T-shirt
a teddy-bear
a tent
a theatre
a thief
a thunderstorm
a toilet
a toothbrush
a traveller's cheque
a two-headed coin
an umbrella
an unexploded bomb
a violin
a window
winter
a zoo

A: X ...
B: ... is like Y
C: ... because ...

Example:

A: Love ...
B: ... is like learning English ...
C: ... because it's fun at first!
Or: because you don't always understand it.
Or: because it takes a lot of time and effort.
Or: because you are always discovering new things.
Or: because it can make you very confused.
Or: ... etc.

32 MAKING SIMILES (3)
Advanced

Jane Revell

X is like Y because ...

What exciting combinations can you make?

X

anger
art
a bride
democracy
depression
failure
fame
fear
freedom
a friend
a good book
the government
home
hope
jealousy
joy
knowledge
life
love
marriage
motherhood
opera
peace
a poem
politics
power
a problem
progress
success
truth
unemployment
war
a woman
work

Y

an ache
an advertisement
alcohol
an Andrew Lloyd Webber musical
Antarctica
an art exhibition
a bad debt
a bald head
a beggar
a beauty contest
boxing
a bra
a broken window-pane
a bruise
a lighted candle
cancer
caviar
a chameleon
champagne
cheap perfume
a chemistry lesson
chickenpox
constipation
cotton-wool
cough mixture
a crossword
a desert
a diet
a disco
a dripping tap
a dustbin
a duster
an earthquake
the Eiffel Tower
an elastic band
an elephant
the environment
an experiment
a fingerprint
a firework
a flood
a funeral
a funfair
a fur coat
gossip
The Grand Canyon
a hedgehog
a heart attack
a hangover
hiccups
a hippopotamus
your horoscope
a hot air balloon
a huge salary
hunger
an ice-rink
an iceberg
jazz
a judge
laughter
learning English
a long queue
a marathon
mathematics
measles
a mosquito
a museum
the number seven
an orphan
a packet of cornflakes
a pair of pyjamas
a paper clip
a Picasso
a picnic
a pillowcase
a poor appetite
a pompon hat
a rainbow
a recipe
a ruler
a runny nose
shampoo
a sneeze
a snowflake
a stick-insect
a straitjacket
a super model
a Swiss cheese
a terrorist
a top hat
a tunnel
a volcano
a whip
willpower
winter
a word-processor

A: X ...
B: ... is like Y
C: ... because ...

Example:

A: Love ...
B: ... is like the Eiffel Tower ...
C: ... because it's a long way up but it's worth it!
Or: because it makes you gasp!
Or: because it's the experience of a lifetime.
Or: because it costs a lot to go up!
Or: because it took a long time to build.
Or: ... etc.

33 SENTENCES FROM TALES

Mario Rinvolucri

1 Then I'll huff and I'll puff	a I smell the blood of an Englishman.
2 So, Chicken Licken	b were three bears and a little girl called Goldilocks.
3 Fee-Fie-Fo-Fum	c ran off to tell the king that the sky was falling in.
4 Run, run, as fast as you can	d and I'll blow your house in.
5 Snow White	e Joe or Joshua or James?
6 Oh, Grandmother,	f and who's eaten it all up?
7 Once upon a time there	g you'll never catch me, I'm the Gingerbread man.
8 Mirror mirror on the wall	h and the seven dwarfs.
9 Is my name Jonathan or	i she ran out of the ballroom.
10 On the stroke of midnight	j what big eyes you've got!
11 Who's been eating my porridge	k who's the fairest one of all?

34 REMEMBERING

Mario Rinvolucri

Memory Questions

1 Do I have a good memory, compared to other people in my family?

2 In general do I tend to remember in pictures, or are sounds, words and feelings more important to me?

3 If I think back to my last holiday, do I feel I am in the place, do I hear sounds and voices vividly, do I have strong, focused colour pictures? Do I have all of these equally strongly?

4 How exactly do I remember phone numbers? Some people know a tapping sequence in their fingers, some people say the number to themselves and some people see the number or the person they are phoning.

5 Can I right now, say my own phone number to myself in ENGLISH? How did I do this?

6 When I meet a person I haven't been with for a long time, do I first recognise them by their voice, by their face or by the way I feel their presence?

7 How, precisely, do I remember the way from one place to another? How do I bring to mind a tube or bus journey I have done only once before?

8 How do I bring back information from the past? Do I see it on the page? Do I hear it? Do I know it some other way?

35 THE WONDERFUL WORLDWIDE NAMES QUIZ

Derek Strange

Can you ...

- name an ocean beginning with **A**? ________________
- name a sort of food beginning with **B**? ________________
- name a country beginning with **C**? ________________
- name a part of a house beginning with **D**? ________________
- name a high mountain beginning with **E**? ________________
- name a day of the week beginning with **F**? ________________
- name a European language beginning with **G**? ________________
- name a type of Japanese car beginning with **H**? ________________
- name an American state beginning with **I**? ________________
- name a month of the year beginning with **J**? ________________
- name a part of the body beginning with **K**? ________________
- name a job beginning with **L**? ________________
- name a large sea beginning with **M**? ________________
- name a planet beginning with **N**? ________________
- name a fruit beginning with **O**? ________________
- name a farm animal beginning with **P**? ________________
- name an Australian state beginning with **Q**? ________________
- name a flower beginning with **R**? ________________
- name a piece of clothing beginning with **S**? ________________
- name a large bird beginning with **T**? ________________
- name an international organization beginning with **U**? ________________
- name a Canadian city beginning with **V**? ________________
- name an alcoholic drink beginning with **W**? ________________
- name a musical instrument beginning with **X**? ________________
- name a colour beginning with **Y**? ________________
- name a country in Africa beginning with **Z**? ________________

36 SOLVE A PROBLEM

Derek Strange

Read the following information and clues to solve the problem. Use the grid below. Put ticks (✓) in the correct boxes to show the names and heights of the girls. Then complete the sentences.

The information and the problem

Alison, Anne, Angela and Abbie all have different surnames. One of them has the surname Bell, one has the surname Carter, one has the surname Davis and one has the surname Edwards. One of them is 160 centimetres tall, one is 170 centimetres tall, one is 175 centimetres tall and the other is 180 centimetres tall.

The problem: *which girl has which surname and how tall is each of the four girls?*

The clues

1 Alison is the shortest person.

2 None of the other girls is taller than Anne.

3 Abbie is not as tall as Angela.

4 Abbie's surname is Davis.

5 The tallest girl is called Edwards.

6 Ms Bell is not 175 centimetres tall.

	Bell	Carter	Davis	Edwards	160 cms	170 cms	175 cms	180 cms
Alison								
Anne								
Angela								
Abbie								

Complete these sentences.

1 Ms Alison ____________ is ____________ centimetres tall.

2 Ms Anne ____________ is ____________ centimetres tall.

3 Ms Angela ____________ is ____________ centimetres tall.

4 Ms Abbie ____________ is ____________ centimetres tall.

37 CONVERSATION ON A TRAIN

Michael Swan and Catherine Walter

Before you start, read through the following notes.

The situation

You are with several other people in a compartment on an old-fashioned railway train. The train is going across Europe and Asia, from Paris to Vladivostok. You have already been travelling for several hours and nobody has spoken. You are bored. Start up a conversation with the others.

To think about

1 Before starting, think about:

who you are

a woman with a child	a Chinese, Russian, French, etc. person
a travelling student	a soldier going home
a plumber, electrician, English teacher, etc.	a prisoner on the run from the police
a film director	a travelling folk singer
a spy	someone who is slightly deaf
a photographer	etc.
a retired schoolteacher	

why you are travelling

for a holiday	on business
for a job	to learn Tai-Chi
to get away from someone	to write a travel book
(boyfriend, girlfriend, family, etc.)	etc.
you won a prize in a competition	

who you are going to see

a penfriend	a famous person (politician, writer, artist, healer)
a family member (brother, sister, uncle, etc.)	as many new people as possible
your boyfriend, girlfriend, husband, wife, etc.	your long lost father, brother, mother, sister, etc.

2 From time to time the train stops at a station. Some people can leave the train; others can get on. Other people may also come into your compartment: ticket-collectors, passport control officers, people selling drinks and sandwiches, etc.

3 Further along the train there is a restaurant car and a bar.

38 STRANGE PRESENTS

Michael Swann and Catherine Walter

a baby tiger	a rubber clock
a dead parrot	a broken vase
an igloo	a stuffed bear
a plastic dog	a bunch of weeds
a Chinese–Swahili dictionary	a bucket with a hole in it
a wooden leg	a packet of used teabags
a bottle of melted snow	a parachute
a bottle of invisible ink	a two-headed coin
a sack of quick-drying cement	a pair of odd socks
a fully-grown ostrich	a bald wig
leather sheets	the back end of a stage horse

39 ONE WORD POEMS

Brian Tomlinson

1 *You are going to read some one word poems. Yes, each poem consists of one word only. As you read each poem below try to make a picture in your mind of what the poem means to you. Then in the space below each word either draw your picture of the poem or write a description of what you saw.*

1 Eggblack	**2 Bookfall**	**3 Crydumb**	
4 Tickchime	**5 Buschain**	**6 Drumstill**	
7 Oneword	**8 Sunwent**	**9 Seagrass**	**10 Lightblue**

2 *Form a group of four and discuss your experience of each poem with the group.*

3 *Now in your group select five of the poems and combine them to form a new five line poem. You can use your own words too if you want to. Write your group poem in the space below.*

(Line 1) ______________________________

(Line 2) ______________________________

(Line 3) ______________________________

(Line 4) ______________________________

(Line 5) ______________________________

40 ASSOCIATIONS
1A (Elementary)

Penny Ur

blue cow nose die shop tomorrow
Singapore elephant
understand money
bad
brown bread book
bus angry
sit
telephone tea monkey
policeman
happily teacher

---

40 ASSOCIATIONS
1B (Elementary)

Penny Ur

exercise computer tree
green
cat quickly car mountain
fall run cold
paper hat
sheep stand
head dollar
America
museum long
fat
stupid sun umbrella

40 ASSOCIATIONS
2A (Intermediate)

Penny Ur

interview
practise
politician
politely
instructions
programme
succeed
introduction
struggle
punish
country
helmet
travel
lifeguard
weight
dangerous
eyebrows
legend
twins
jewellery
realistic
pollution
planet
comfortably

---

40 ASSOCIATIONS
2B (Intermediate)

Penny Ur

old-fashioned
gravity
disease
sweetly
official
truth
destroy
melt
decide
powerful
experience
refuse
sunbathing
humour
mild
government
disappointed
valley
responsible
competition
bored
warn
diary
iceberg

40 ASSOCIATIONS
3A (Advanced)

Penny Ur

wink legal customer compulsory monument reservation contrast metaphorically progress rocket branch smash concur wholesale bisect jubilee protective hierarchy stifle disgraceful cattle embrace

40 ASSOCIATIONS
3B (Advanced)

Penny Ur

correspondence spiral fugitive fictional tentacle frost smouldering punctuation footprint artificial creative message platoon forgery freight collectively compass ozone layer cathedral ethnic group mutual symmetrical continental flutter

41 I SYMPATHIZE

Penny Ur

Questions	Sympathizers
1 *What is your favourite colour? Choose one of the following:* red, yellow, blue, green, orange, purple	1 _____ 2 _____ 3 _____ 4 _____ 5 _____ 6 _____
2 *Which animal do you like best? Choose one of the following:* dog, cat, monkey, horse, sheep, elephant, mouse	1 _____ 2 _____ 3 _____ 4 _____ 5 _____ 6 _____
3 *Which household job do you hate most? Choose from the following:* washing dishes, cleaning floors, cleaning windows, washing clothes, tidying up, dusting	1 _____ 2 _____ 3 _____ 4 _____ 5 _____ 6 _____
4 *What kind of people do you envy most? Choose from the following:* rich people, good-looking people, professionally successful people, popular people, famous people	1 _____ 2 _____ 3 _____ 4 _____ 5 _____ 6 _____
5 *What kind of films do you like best? Choose from the following:* thrillers, romantic films, comedies, dramas, horror films, documentaries, action films, musicals	1 _____ 2 _____ 3 _____ 4 _____ 5 _____ 6 _____

42 LOST PROPERTY

Peter Viney

Student A

You are going to role-play a conversation with Student B.

You're at the Lost Property Office of the Sandbourne Bus Company.
(Student B is a clerk there.)

You were on a number 38 bus.

It left the town centre at 3.15.

It arrived at the sports stadium at 3.45.

You left a green bag on the seat.

There was a kilo of Camembert cheese in the bag.

When you got on the bus, the driver complained about the strong smell of the cheese.

You don't live in Sandbourne. You're only here for the day.

Student B

You are going to role-play a conversation with Student A.

You work at the Lost Property Office of the Sandbourne Bus Company.

It's 5.25. You finish work at 5.30.

The office closes at 5.30.

You're meeting someone at 5.35.

You have a headache.

You haven't got the lost property Student A asks for.

Ask for information about the lost property.

The bus driver of the number 38 bus finishes work at 6 p.m.

Suggest that the passenger returns tomorrow.

42 LOST PROPERTY (continued)

Peter Viney

Class activity

Watch two students (A and B) doing a role-play, and complete this form while you're watching. You can check more than one box for each line. Read it carefully before you begin!

1 I thought Student A was (☐ aggressive ☐ annoyed ☐ polite ☐ pleasant.)

2 I thought Student B was (☐ unhelpful ☐ helpful ☐ friendly ☐ rude.)

3 Student A (☐ smiled a lot ☐ didn't smile ☐ looked angry.)

4 Student B (☐ smiled a lot ☐ didn't smile ☐ looked angry.)

5 Student A (☐ stood still ☐ moved around ☐ waved his/her arms.)

6 Student B (☐ stood still ☐ moved around ☐ waved his/her arms.)

7 Student A felt (☐ worse ☐ better ☐ the same) at the end of the conversation.

8 Student B felt (☐ worse ☐ better ☐ the same) at the end of the conversation.

9 I thought Student A was (☐ right ☐ wrong) to behave as (s)he did.

10 I thought Student B was (☐ right ☐ wrong) to behave as (s)he did.

Class activity

Watch two students (A and B) doing a role-play, and complete this form while you're watching. You can check more than one box for each line. Read it carefully before you begin!

1 I thought Student A was (☐ aggressive ☐ annoyed ☐ polite ☐ pleasant.)

2 I thought Student B was (☐ unhelpful ☐ helpful ☐ friendly ☐ rude.)

3 Student A (☐ smiled a lot ☐ didn't smile ☐ looked angry.)

4 Student B ☐ smiled a lot ☐ didn't smile ☐ looked angry.)

5 Student A (☐ stood still ☐ moved around ☐ waved his/her arms.)

6 Student B (☐ stood still ☐ moved around ☐ waved his/her arms.)

7 Student A felt (☐ worse ☐ better ☐ the same) at the end of the conversation.

8 Student B felt (☐ worse ☐ better ☐ the same) at the end of the conversation.

9 I thought Student A was (☐ right ☐ wrong) to behave as (s)he did.

10 I thought Student B was (☐ right ☐ wrong) to behave as (s)he did.

43 FIND THE HIDDEN SENTENCES

Peter Watcyn-Jones

There are eight sentences hidden in the following grid. See if you can find them. Write your answers at the bottom of the page. You can only move one square at a time.

1 Anne	3 We	4 The	play	tennis	up	8 He	love
and	capital	usually	on	gave	smoking	met	three
of	her	Friday.	wine.	6 James	he	two	his
Indonesia	is	sister	of	7 Do	you	years	wife
2 French	are	Jakarta.	to	lot	want	at	ago.
dogs	people	twins.	a	animals,	a	to	know
is	likes	drink	love	party.	especially	for	a
to	saw	5 I	go	for	dogs.	secret?	train

1 Anne ________ ________ sister ________ ________.

2 French ________ ________ a ________ ________ ________.

3 We ________ ________ ________ on ________.

4 The ________ ________ ________ ________ Jakarta.

5 I ________ ________ ________ dogs.

6 James ________ ________ ________ two ________ ________.

7 Do ________ ________ to ________ ________ ________?

8 He ________ ________ ________ at ________ ________.

44 DO YOU GET EASILY CONFUSED?

Peter Watcyn-Jones

Work in pairs or groups of three. You have a time-limit of 10 minutes to complete the following.

		Points
1	If the letter Z appears anywhere before this comma, cross it out. If not, cross it out in this word: ZEBRA.	
2	Now if the word 'car' appears in scared, draw a cross here ___________. Otherwise draw a triangle.	
3	And by the way, if the letter Z is number 26 in the alphabet, what does F + T add up to? Write your answer here: ___________	
4	Write OCEAN here ___________ if the word starts with a vowel. If not, write the last four letters of the alphabet.	
5	Underline the second word after 'the' in this sentence.	
6	If G is the seventh letter of the alphabet, then don't write the number 22 in this gap ___________ but write the number 65 instead.	
7	Look at instructions 1–3 above. Write down here how many times the word 'the' is used. ___________	
8	If the answer to the question 'What is the capital of Wales?' is Belfast, write ROME in this gap ___________. Otherwise, write BANANA.	
9	Draw a circle around the third word in this sentence and a line under the last word in the next sentence.	
10	Write HELP in this gap ___________ if a woman is sometimes taller than a man.	
11	Next, write the answer to the question 'What day is it today?' in this gap if there are more than 23 words in this sentence. ___________	
12	Now, if you've had enough, write NO MORE in the gap at the end of this sentence. Otherwise, write NO MORE. ___________	
	Total	

45 SAME WORD – DIFFERENT MEANING (1)

Intermediate | **Peter Watcyn-Jones**

ash	ball	bark
bill	blind	boil
book	bow	bridge
change	chest	coach
date	fair	lean
light	match	palm
sole	spring	stamp
train	watch	wave

45 SAME WORD – DIFFERENT MEANING (2)

Upper Intermediate/Advanced

Peter Watcyn-Jones

admit	bear	bolt
charge	conduct	court
desert	draught	faint
fan	fence	grave
hide	leave	litter
note	private	rear
refuse	row	sentence
sound	temple	well

46 EXPLAIN THE WORDS (1)
Intermediate

Peter Watcyn-Jones

an *anonymous* letter	a *corrupt* police officer	to *abolish* nuclear weapons
a *damp* cellar	a *huge* garden	to *applaud* loudly
a dusty *attic*	an *invisible* line	to *hum* a song
a clever *barrister*	a *lame* horse	to *hijack* a plane
a frightening *earthquake*	a *remote* village	to *inherit* £25,000
a *second-hand* car	a favourite *nephew*	a *shabby* coat
to *tan* easily	a cold *draught*	a *waterproof* jacket
a £10,000 *ransom*	an *urgent* message	to *demolish* a cinema

46 EXPLAIN THE WORDS (2)

Upper intermediate/Advanced

Peter Watcyn-Jones

a *skinny* secretary	a *former* president	to look around *furtively*
an *uninhabited* island	a black *trilby*	a *hostile* reception
an *inarticulate* lecturer	an *ingenious* idea	a *long-winded* speech
a *terrible* hangover	to *loathe* pop music	an annoying *nosy parker*
a *pushy* person	a *monotonous* job	a *bilingual* teacher
a *fragrant* perfume	a *dog-eared* book	an *irate* parent
a *discourteous* teenager	an *illicit* love affair	to work *diligently*
a *weird* experience	a *husky* voice	a *boisterous* game

47 THE DEFINITION GAME
Student A

Peter Watcyn-Jones

Try to find what these words are.
Ask: What's number (1)?

1		O			L						
2			N			Y					
3			T			–	H				
4		R				A		T			
5	S			P							
6		R				T					
7			T				S				
8	D				B					N	
9				F							
10			C			T					

Now try to explain:

1 divorce (n)
2 emigrate (vb)
3 biography (n)
4 cheerful (adj)
5 brochure (n)
6 choir (n)
7 exaggerate (vb)
8 boring (adj)
9 crawl (vb)
10 voluntary (adj)

e.g. (No 3)
It's a (*noun*). It's a person's life story, but written by someone else, etc.

47 THE DEFINITION GAME
Student B

Peter Watcyn-Jones

Try to explain:

1 complain (vb)

2 lonely (adj)

3 hitch-hike (vb)

4 pregnant (adj)

5 slippery (adj)

6 arrest (vb)

7 witness (n)

8 disobedient (adj)

9 profit (n)

10 dictator (n)

e.g. (No 3)
It's a *(verb)* and it's what you might do when you can't afford the bus fare or the train fare, etc.

Now, try to find what these words are.
Ask: *What's number (1)?*

1

	I			R		

2

E						T	

3

		O		R				Y

4

		E			F		

5

	R			H			

6

	H			

7

E				G					E

8

		R			G

9

C				L

10

	O			N				Y

48 DRAWING A SNIPPET
Student A

Tessa Woodward

Read the following text. It's a true story from a newspaper.

> Don Raddeli, 57, an electrician, was fined £75 at Canterbury, Kent yesterday for wiring up his tumble drier to a streetlamp outside his house.

1 Check any words you need in a dictionary or ask your teacher.
2 On a separate piece of paper make a drawing of what happened.
3 Give your drawing to your partner.
((S)he will try to guess the story from your drawing.)

---

48 DRAWING A SNIPPET
Student B

Tessa Woodward

Read the following text. It's a true story from a newspaper.

> A father in Pennsylvania, USA, left his 3-month-old son in a portable car seat on the roof of his car while he strapped his older sister inside and drove off. When he reached 50 m.p.h., he heard a sliding noise and, looking in his mirror, saw the baby falling into the road. The boy was crying a little but was unhurt.

1 Check any words you need in a dictionary or ask your teacher.
2 On a separate piece of paper make a drawing of what happened.
3 Give your drawing to your partner.
((S)he will try to guess the story from your drawing.)

49 MODERN MYTHS

Andrew Wright and Julia Dudas

THE ANGORA RABBIT

Did I tell you about the angora rabbit in Manchester? No?! Well, it's an amazing story! A friend of a friend of mine told it to me. He said it was true! Anyway, this couple in Manchester didn't have any children so they bought a rabbit, an angora rabbit, you know, the one with long white hair and little red eyes like panasonic power lights. They loved this rabbit. They kissed it and cuddled it and called it sweetheart and all that sort of thing.

Anyway, the couple next door had a small dog, you know, the sort that bites postmen in the ankle. And they said, If our dog ever gets that rabbit it's going to be a very dead rabbit.

Anyway, one day they came downstairs and saw their dog in the garden going, Grrrr! Grrrr! So they went into the garden and found it had got a very dead rabbit. The neighbours weren't in; the car wasn't in the drive so the people with the dog took the rabbit inside the house and put it on the kitchen table.

'They are going to be so upset if they know our dog killed their rabbit!'

'Why don't we get another one? They might not notice the difference!'

So they raced off to the local pet shop and bought one. It looked just the same to them. They raced back and put it into its hutch and then went back home.

A little while later the couple came home, drove their car up the drive, stopped, got out and went across the garden crying. The couple with the dog saw them. Suddenly they stopped and began to scream and hold each other! The couple with the dog ran out and said over the garden fence,

'Is everything all right?'

'No! It's the rabbit!'

'What's wrong with it?'

'It's alive!'

'What's wrong with that?'

'Well, it died yesterday and we buried it!'

50 SOAP FACES

Andrew Wright and Julia Dudas